Bibliografische Information der Deutschen Nationalbibliothek

Die Deutsche Nationalbibliothek verzeichnet diese Publikation in der
Deutschen Nationalbibliografie; detaillierte bibliografische Daten sind
im Internet über http://dnb.d-nb.de abrufbar.

ISBN 978-3-8325-2463-0

Logos Verlag Berlin GmbH
Comeniushof, Gubener Str. 47,
10243 Berlin
Tel.: +49 (0)30 42 85 10 90
Fax: +49 (0)30 42 85 10 92
INTERNET: http://www.logos-verlag.de

Multithreaded Programming and Execution Models for Reconfigurable Hardware

Dissertation

A thesis submitted to the
Faculty of Computer Science, Electrical Engineering, and Mathematics
of the
University of Paderborn
in partial fulfillment of the requirements for the
degree of *Dr. rer. nat.*

by

Enno Lübbert Egge Lübbers

Paderborn, Germany
Date of submission: 10.02.2010

Supervisor:
Prof. Dr. Marco Platzner

Reviewers:
Prof. Dr. Marco Platzner
Prof. Dr. David Andrews
Prof. Dr. Franz J. Rammig

Additional members of the oral examination committee:
Prof. Dr. Sybille Hellebrand
Prof. Dr. André Brinkmann

Date of submission:
February 10, 2010

Date of public examination:
March 25, 2010

Acknowledgements

My first and foremost thanks go to my advisor Prof. Marco Platzner, for supporting my research and providing me with an exceptional research environment. I have greatly benefited from his guidance, experience, and advice during my work in his group and very much value our continued collaboration.

Furthermore, I would like to thank:

- Prof. David Andrews, for our rewarding and encouraging collaboration, and also for serving as reviewer for my dissertation.

- Prof. Franz Rammig, for serving as reviewer for my dissertation.

- Prof. Sybille Hellebrand and Prof. André Brinkmann, for serving on my oral examination committee.

- My colleagues Tobias Beisel, Stephanie Drzevitzky, Heiner Giefers, Mariusz Grad, Markus Happe, Paul Kaufmann, Tobias Kenter, Björn Meyer, Christian Plessl, Lars Schäfers, and Tobias Schumacher, for helpful and motivating discussions as well as constructive criticism and valuable feedback on many aspects of my work.

- My student assistants Andreas Agne and Robert Meiche, as well as the Bachelor, Master, and Diploma students I supervised, who helped evaluating a considerable part of my concepts and contributed significantly to the ReconOS infrastructure.

- The Deutsche Forschungsgemeinschaft (DFG), for funding the priority program "Rekonfigurierbare Rechensysteme" (SPP1148); and my co-researchers within the SPP as well as Jason Agron and Ariane Keller, for fruitful discussions on many aspects of reconfigurable computing.

Finally, I would also like to thank my family, in particular my parents Wiebke and Enno, my brother Eiken and my sister Frauke, for their care, encouragement, and inspiration; and Diana Meise, for her patience and support.

Abstract

Rising logic densities together with the inclusion of dedicated processor cores have increasingly promoted reconfigurable logic devices, such as FPGAs, from traditional application areas such as glue logic, emulation, and prototyping to powerful implementation platforms for complete reconfigurable systems-on-chip. The combination of fast CPU cores and fine-grained reconfigurable logic allows designers to map both sequential, control-dominated code and highly parallel data-centric computations onto a single programmable device. However, traditional design techniques that view specialized hardware circuits as passive coprocessors are ill-suited for programming these reconfigurable computers. In particular, the programming models for software (running on an embedded operating system) and digital hardware (synthesized to an FPGA) lack commonalities which hinders design space exploration and severely impairs the potential for code re-use. Moreover, the promising feature of partial reconfiguration available in modern SRAM-based FPGAs has yet to be embraced by a pervasive programming paradigm.

In this thesis, we present fundamental work in the new area of multithreaded programming of reconfigurable logic devices. We propose an execution environment called ReconOS that is based on existing embedded operating systems and extends the multithreaded programming model—already established and highly successful in the software domain—to reconfigurable hardware. Using threads and common synchronization and communication services as an abstraction layer, our design and execution platforms allow for the creation of portable and flexible multithreaded HW/SW applications for CPU/FPGA systems.

This work introduces the ReconOS programming model and its run-time environment, discusses its implications for the design of hardware components, and introduces non-preemptive and cooperative mechanisms for run-time sharing of reconfigurable resources through partial reconfiguration techniques integrated into the operating system. It presents implementations based on modern platform FPGAs and the software host operating systems eCos and Linux, quantifies time and area overheads of the proposed mechanisms and, finally, demonstrates the feasibility and the benefits of the multithreading design approach with several case studies.

Zusammenfassung

Sowohl die zunehmende Integrationsdichte moderner digitaler Logik als auch die Verschmelzung von programmierbarer Logik mit Mikroprozessoren haben dazu geführt, dass FPGAs zunehmend aus ihren klassischen Rollen als Verbindungslogik, Emulations- und Prototypisierungsplattform ausbrechen und zur Umsetzung vollständiger rekonfigurierbarer "Systems-on-Chip" genutzt werden. Die Verbindung von leistungsfähigen Prozessorkernen und feingranularer rekonfigurierbarer Logik ermöglicht es, sowohl sequentielle und kontrolllastige als auch hochgradig datenparallele Berechnungen auf einer gemeinsamen Plattform durchzuführen. Konventionelle Entwurfsmethoden integrieren spezialisierte Hardware-Module oft als passive Co-Prozessoren und eignen sich daher schlecht zur Programmierung dieser hybriden rekonfigurierbaren Computer. Insbesondere überlappen sich die Programmiermodelle für Software (üblicherweise auf einem eingebetteten Betriebssystem ausgeführt) und digitaler Hardware (implementiert als programmierte Schaltungen eines FPGAs) nicht ausreichend, was das Potential für die Wiederverwendung von Modulen und die flexible Nutzung des HW/SW-Entwurfsraumes stark schmälert. Darüber hinaus findet die vielversprechende Möglichkeit zur partiellen Rekonfiguration, wie sie moderne SRAM-basierte FPGAs bieten, bisher keine Entsprechung in einem verbreiteten Entwurfsverfahren.

In der vorliegenden Arbeit stellen wir ein neuartiges und grundlegendes Konzept der Programmierung von Hardware-Modulen als Threads für programmierbare Hardware vor. Wir zeigen eine Ausführungsumgebung namens ReconOS, die auf bestehenden eingebetteten Betriebssystemen basiert und das Multithreading-Programmiermodell, das bereits verbreitet und erfolgreich in Software-Umgebungen eingesetzt wird, auch auf rekonfigurierbare Hardware anwendet. Mittels Threads und gemeinsamen Synchronisations- und Kommunikations-Mechanismen als Abstraktionsschicht erlaubt unsere Entwurfs- und Ausführungsumgebung die Erstellung von portablen und flexiblen Hardware-/Software-Anwendungen für CPU/FPGA-Systeme.

Diese Arbeit diskutiert das ReconOS-Programmiermodell und die zugehörige Laufzeitumgebung und ihre Auswirkungen auf den Entwurf von Hardware-Threads und zeigt nicht-preemptive und kooperative Verfahren zur Nutzung der partiellen Rekonfiguration. Wir präsentieren Implementierungen auf Basis moderner Plattform-FPGAs und den Betriebssystemen eCos und Linux, quantifizieren Flächenbedarf und Latenzen der vorgestellten Verfahren und demonstrieren die Anwendbarkeit und die Vorteile des Multithreading-Ansatzes anhand mehrerer Fallstudien.

Contents

List of Figures

List of Tables

CHAPTER 1

Introduction

Choosing the right processing architecture for an embedded system has always been a matter of balancing objectives and constraints. The spectrum of processing elements available for the implementation of an embedded system is delimited by flexible, general-purpose processors and dedicated application-specific integrated circuits (ASICs), with specialized and programmable architectures like digital signal processors (DSPs), application-specific instruction-set processors (ASIPs) and field-programmable gate arrays (FPGAs) in between. Each class of processing element brings with it a separate, individual set of programming models and tools that accounts for the specifics of the particular technology. Where previously, selecting the appropriate execution environment was often considered a simple trade-off between unit cost and performance, the actual decision space becomes somewhat more complex when taking design aspects into account.

Recent embedded systems require significant computational resources, e.g., for signal processing, streaming, compression, or cryptographic applications, while at the same time being constrained in cost, energy consumption, as well as development time. The rising cost of manufacturing custom circuits in current process technologies and the increasing power consumption of modern high-performance general-purpose processors have driven a demand for off-the-shelf components (or *platforms*) with low or at least scalable energy consumption, narrowing the field of available processing solutions for embedded systems to embedded processors, DSPs, and FPGAs. A result of this trend is the recent integration of reconfigurable logic with microprocessors, DSP elements, and other dedicated components into *platform FPGAs*. According to the promises

1

of the manufacturers, these devices combine the best of both the sequential and parallel processing worlds. Platform FPGAs certainly promote the application areas of reconfigurable logic from glue logic and ASIC prototyping toward self-contained systems-on-chip (SoCs).

However, the tools and programming models for reconfigurable logic devices have not kept up with the rising complexities presented by these devices. Traditional design techniques that view specialized hardware circuits as passive coprocessors are ill-suited for programming reconfigurable computers. In particular, the programming models for software—running on an embedded operating system (OS)—and digital hardware—synthesized to an FPGA—lack commonalities which hinders design space exploration and severely impairs the potential for code re-use.

Another promising but under-appreciated feature of some reconfigurable logic devices that is so far hardly acknowledged outside of the academic world is *dynamic partial reconfiguration* (DPR)—the ability of a hardware device to replace a part of its circuitry with another during run-time without interrupting the execution of the remaining logic, as opposed to full or static configuration of the entire device. In theory, DPR allows the time-multiplexing of logic area, similar to the context switching capabilities of a microprocessor, a mechanism also called *hardware multitasking*.

While the use of reconfigurable devices with static configurations is well understood and supported through tools provided by the manufacturers, generation and management of dynamic partial reconfiguration is still a very active research topic. As opposed to software compilation flows or hardware synthesis and implementation cycles, there is no established end-to-end flow for generating both the run-time environment and the actual configurations for partially reconfigurable devices from a single application description.

This thesis presents fundamental work in the field of programming hybrid hardware/software systems based on reconfigurable hardware. We have developed a novel programming paradigm and run-time environment for modern platform FPGAs that covers both sequential software and parallel hardware with a single unified programming model. Our approach is based on multithreaded programming, as widely used in the embedded software domain, in combination with a robust operating system kernel. We promote hardware modules from their traditional role as passive coprocessors to being regarded as *hardware threads* on the same level as software threads, with access to the same operating system resources. Through the use of a unified programming model and the subsequent increase of code re-use and simplified design space exploration we can effectively raise the design productivity of hybrid hardware/software systems targeted at platform FPGAs to a level previously only achieved for software-based systems. At the same time, our run-time environment leverages the partial reconfiguration capabilities of platform FPGAs to further exploit the thread-level parallelism made explicit by the programming model.

The following Section 1.1 outlines important research topics related to programming models for reconfigurable computers. Section 1.2 lists the contribution of this dissertation to the state-of-the-art in theory and implementation of programming models for embedded hardware/software co-design. Finally, Section 1.3 outlines the structure of this thesis.

1.1 Research Areas in Embedded Reconfigurable Computing

The rise both in device density as well as in application, architecture and algorithm complexity is constantly expanding the scope of reconfigurable computing systems. While today's software engineers struggle with the efficient exploitation of homogeneous multiprocessors, most reconfigurable computers offer a vastly heterogeneous execution environment. The extensive design space offered by platform FPGAs is currently not matched by design tools and programming models, making a complex reconfigurable SoC design difficult to handle. In the software world, rising design complexity brought about by increasing memory sizes and processing speed was met by standard libraries, scalable programming paradigms, and eventually operating systems providing a suitable execution environment. In embedded reconfigurable computing, these developments are still in progress, as the application areas of FPGAs move from simple glue logic and ASIC prototyping platforms toward complete, self-contained systems-on-chip.

In the following, we summarize important research topics related to the programming of complex embedded reconfigurable systems.

Operating System Integration of Reconfigurable Hardware

The fundamental concept behind an operating system is to group common functionality and provide it as a service to an application. Instead of integrating identical run-time functionalities into every application module, it is more efficient to develop central—and possibly more general—implementations together with a standard interface or application programmer interface (API), and group these implementations in an operating system. This decreases the system's resource requirements, increases productivity through defined interfaces and possible code re-use, enables portability of applications across different execution environments, and simplifies debugging by leveraging OS-provided monitoring and profiling services.

Given the increasing system complexity that is made possible by rising reconfigurable device densities, operating system support for reconfigurable logic is a popular research topic. While pursuing the same goals as a software operating system, and consequently heavily borrowing concepts from the software domain, operating systems for reconfigurable hardware face additional problems. Management of reconfigurable modules is more complex than managing software threads, with problems ranging from reconfiguration-aware scheduling [34] to geometric placement [43]. The communication between hardware modules and the operating system requires additional specialized hardware modules [109] and OS kernel modifications [100, 112]. In fact, as a reconfigurable SoC resembles a heterogeneous multi-core system unlike the target architectures for existing, software-based operating systems, it is an interesting research topic to find out which OS services realistically translate to the reconfigurable domain at all.

Another direction of research in operating systems and reconfigurable logic is the implementation of core OS services in the reconfigurable fabric itself. By using dedicated logic for certain OS functions, such as the scheduler or synchronization primitives [16, 64], the system can be optimized for certain requirements, such as low jitter. Other more high-level functionality, such as cryptographic functions, can be offered as an operating system service to applications [63] and benefit from a hardware implementation. Determining a suitable hardware/software partitioning would in this case extend from application modules to the operating system.

Programming Model

Reconfigurable logic in embedded systems is usually applied with the goals of reducing development cycle time, lengthening product life, and providing in-the-field updatability. FPGAs provide a feasible implementation vehicle for flexible system architectures, combining processing elements and application-specific peripherals in a system-on-chip. In this development model, hardware modules are usually specified in a low-level hardware description language, connected to the system's memory bus, and programmed through a dedicated, memory-mapped register interface. This traditional passive coprocessor model does not scale well with the rising device complexity, and hampers productivity by requiring architecture-specific, inflexible and intransparent interface code. Additionally, complex bus protocols are not well suited to providing an efficient and flexible interface for connecting partially reconfigurable modules.

Using higher-level abstractions for modeling reconfigurable hardware to increase portability and scaleability is a viable approach [21, 46, 81, 93], but often faces difficulties in modeling implicit parallelism [41] and integration with dynamically reconfigurable systems [120], and thus frequently incurs a significant performance loss compared to a hand-crafted implementation. There is considerable commercial interest in generating parallel hardware descriptions from (augmented) sequential programming languages, such as C [27, 56]. On the other hand, system-level approaches, such as multithreading together with heterogeneous multi-cores [15] are also actively being researched. These approaches often combine and integrate with an operating system, as discussed above.

Dynamic Partial Reconfiguration

The dynamic partial reconfiguration capabilities of SRAM-based FPGAs [72] open up many possibilites in different research directions. This feature can be used for hardware virtualization [42], fault-tolerance [22], or even hardware circuit evolution [61]. There are numerous projects serving as examples of commercial application of run-time or partial reconfigurability, such as video mixing and general video processing (e.g., post-processing, denoising and color correction) of high-resolution video data [1, 38], cognitive and software defined radio [53, 60], multi-standard radio transceivers [30], and visualization of medical data [75]. However, being more of a side-product of the FPGA's configuration infrastructure than a marketable product feature, the manufacturer support both by tools and hardware cores is somewhat lacking. As a consequence, DPR has a steep learning curve and requires a significant engineering effort to apply, and thus the uptake and the visibility of the technology within the industry as a whole is rather limited when compared to traditional uses of reconfigurable technology. In turn, there is neither an obvious high-profile application for DPR, nor is the demand for supporting infrastructures, tools, or suitable programming models one of the industry's highest priorities. In view of this hen-and-egg problem, the task of developing DPR methods, tool flows, and applications has been taken up by academia.

The research area of dynamic partial reconfiguration is overlapping considerably with the OS integration of reconfigurable logic, since the task of managing reconfigurable portions of a hardware design involves synchronization of concurrently executing modules and resource management techniques. The reconfiguration times, which exceed context switch times exhibited by CPUs by several orders of magnitude, are a major bottleneck and significantly limit the scope of applications suitable for dynamic partial reconfiguration. Low-level techniques for reducing bitstream size [94] and increasing reconfiguration data throughput [28], as well as reconfiguration-aware scheduling techniques [33] are needed for efficient application of partial reconfiguration in embedded systems.

1.2 Contributions of This Thesis

The main contribution of this thesis is a novel method to transparently support both hardware and software threads within dynamically reconfigurable hardware through a unified programming model and its integration with established embedded operating system environments. In particular, we make the following contributions to the state-of-the-art in programming hybrid CPU/FPGA systems:

- We have developed a unified, multithreaded programming model for both software threads (running on the system's CPU) and hardware threads (mapped to the reconfigurable fabric), and an associated execution model for modern platform FPGAs. By interfacing with existing multithreading-capable operating system kernels, these models allow hardware modules to access the same operating system services for communication and synchronization as their software counterparts. Thus, communication partners do not need to know whether their peers are threads executing on a CPU or modules mapped to an FPGA. This greatly simplifies design-space exploration during the co-design of otherwise complex to parametrize hardware/software systems, and enables productivity increases through standard interfaces and code re-use.

- In order to support operating system calls from within hardware modules, we have implemented a function library and a methodology for the design of hardware threads that allow low-level synchronization and communication from within hardware threads written in VHDL. By augmenting a VHDL description with a structured state machine description we support both newly created hardware threads as well as turning existing legacy hardware cores into threads. Together with a specialized hardware module, the operating system interface (OSIF), we provide a method to structure a hardware thread's operating system interactions very similarly to the writing of a software thread, while maintaining a VHDL description's potential for data-parallel processing.

- We have added support for hardware threads to the widely used software operating system kernels eCos and Linux. Hardware threads are represented in the operating system through a controlling software thread, the *delegate thread*, which acts as a proxy and executes operating system calls on behalf of their hardware threads. In this way, our operating system provides support for existing software and standard I/O interfaces, as well as a seamless and portable integration of hardware threads.

- Taking the unique requirements of reconfigurable hardware threads in a multithreaded environment into account, we have developed a cooperative multitasking technique for hardware threads. Contrary to multitasking solutions for software systems, which often employ preemptive techniques, reconfigurable hardware faces difficulties with preemptive multitasking. As an alternative, we have developed and implemented an OS supported infrastructure for allowing hardware threads to time-share reconfigurable resources using non-preemptive and cooperative scheduling approaches.

- To reduce the complexity of designing multithreaded hardware software systems, which is a challenging task using current vendor tools, we have developed an end-to-end tool flow from application description to executable and partial bit streams. This flow integrates with existing design tools for reconfigurable SoC design and supports both static and dynamically reconfigurable hardware threads. We have devised a novel incremental development style for hybrid hardware/software systems that allows for straightforward design space exploration regarding the hardware/software partitioning. At the individual stages of this tool flow, we provide module and system simulation tools as well as monitoring and testing mechanisms, which aid in debugging and profiling complex co-designed applications.

The work presented in this thesis was conducted as part of the Priority Programme (SPP) 1148 "Reconfigurable Computing Systems" of the German National Science Foundation (DFG), the results of which are summarized in [12]. Of the other works within the SPP, the following are of particular interest in relation to this thesis, as they cover complementary research areas both in high-level hardware design and synthesis as well as in low-level analysis and implementation of reconfigurable architectures:

Schallenberg et. al.: *POLYDYN– Object-oriented modeling and synthesis.* In this work, an object-oriented modeling approach was developed based on SystemC, that also addresses DPR effects and automatic system synthesis, albeit without software integration or operating system support.

Rullmann and Merker: *Design Methods and Tools for Improved Partial Dynamic Reconfiguration.* This project investigated the reduction of partial bitstream sizes by analyzing common components of different configurations within a high-level synthesis (HLS) flow. Together, we developed an experimental prototype and demonstrator [4], where an image processing application's hardware threads were synthesized using the HLS approach and then executed together with software threads on our execution environment.

Montealegre and Rammig: *Dynamic Partial Reconfiguration by Means of Algorithmic Skeletons.* Here, the potential of algorithmic skeletons was investigated as a means for effectively partitioning parallel applications on a variety of reconfigurable target architectures.

Angermeier et. al.: *The Erlangen Slot Machine (ESM).* The authors of this work designed and implemented a communication and reconfiguration infrastructure based on a custom FPGA board design, which is aimed at simplifying the design of partially reconfigurable systems on the physical level. The ESM is one of the supported target platforms of our work, and provided the implementation target of the demonstrator presented in [4].

Ahmadinia et. al.: *Optimization Methods for Module Scheduling and Placement.* This project deals with efficiently placing and scheduling reconfigurable modules within a reconfigurable device in order to reduce fragmentation effects.

1.3 Thesis Structure

This section outlines the structure of this thesis.

Chapter 2 introduces reconfigurable devices and platforms and the established techniques for programming them. The chapter provides the necessary background for the remainder of this thesis and presents related work in operating systems for reconfigurable hardware.

Chapter 3 outlines the concept and key ideas of the multithreaded reconfigurable operating system that forms the basis for the contributions of this thesis. It identifies design objectives and summarizes the programming model and architecture, which the next two chapters build on.

Chapter 4 describes the mechanisms used to model hardware components mapped to reconfigurable logic as hardware threads together with the low-level communication and synchronization methods used to link hardware threads with the operating system kernel.

Chapter 5 gives a detailed description of the methods and tools used for assembling and implementing the execution environment for our multithreaded operating system. It also presents tools and mechanisms for simulation, monitoring, and debugging of a complex, multithreaded CPU/FPGA system.

Chapter 6 introduces hardware multitasking concepts for reconfigurable hardware, and describes their implementation and integration with our multithreaded programming and execution model. The chapter covers scheduling, context save and restore techniques, as well as an overview of the employed tools for generating a partially reconfigurable system.

Chapter 7 takes the concepts and implementations described in the previous chapters and experimentally evaluates the involved overheads and attainable performance with prototype implementations of both synthetic and real-world applications. These case studies also serve to demonstrate non-quantifiable features of our approach, such as portability and ease of design-space exploration.

Chapter 8 finally summarizes the results and contributions of this thesis, draws conclusions and gives suggestions for future research.

CHAPTER 2

Background and Related Work

This chapter provides an introduction to programmable logic devices and reviews associated work on programming models and operating systems. This information will be essential for the understanding and contextual placement of the remainder of this thesis.

In Section 2.1, we give a short overview of programmable logic devices and FPGAs, in particular, as they are the targeted platform for the concepts presented in this thesis. We also look at current tools and techniques for partial reconfiguration of FPGAs. Section 2.2 reviews existing programming models targeted at reconfigurable logic, and Section 2.3 presents related work on operating system concepts for reconfigurable devices.

2.1 Programmable Logic Devices

Programmable logic devices (PLDs) are a class of integrated circuits whose functionality is not determined during the production process of the device, but can be programmed by the end user. Depending on their size and the degree of their programmability, PLDs cover applications from simple combinational glue-logic to complete programmable systems-on-chip. The distinction between PLDs and other types of integrated circuits is sometimes not clearly cut. Some classes of PLDs are similar to a partially pre-layouted ASIC, where the programmability is achieved through the specification of a small subset of the chip's layers, while other more coarse-grain-programmable devices are closer to an ASIP. In the following, we consider the term *programmable logic* to be specific to hardware devices whose logic structure can be modified by the user.

Many programmable logic devices can be reprogrammed multiple times, making them ideal for low-volume applications, as a prototyping and emulation platform in the ASIC design process, and for education and research in digital logic design. More advanced uses of PLDs require run-time or partial reconfiguration techniques which are only available within the more complex types such as FPGAs.

After briefly touching simple and complex PLDs (SPLDs and CPLDs), we will mainly focus on the architecture and associated design flow of FPGAs, as they represent the primary target and implementation platform of the work presented in this thesis.

2.1.1 SPLDs and CPLDs

Simple programmable logic devices (SPLDs) allow the implementation of digital logic functions represented in a sum-of-products form. They are typically composed of two logic planes, an AND- and an OR-plane, with one or both of them being programmable. Figure 2.1(a) shows an SPLD with four inputs, four outputs and a programmable OR plane (programmable array logic, PAL). As evident from the layout, the complexity of the implementable logic functions is limited by the size of the interconnection structure of the device. SPLDs have frequently been used as glue logic and interface modules, replacing multiple small- and medium-scale integrated (SSI/MSI) circuits, as they provide higher packaging density and lower power consumption.

Complex programmable logic devices (CPLDs) are basically a collection of SPLDs, connected by a programmable interconnection network. Together with sequential storage elements (registers), they allow the implementation of more complex and stateful computational elements. A CPLD comprises a number of *function blocks*, which in turn are composed of several SPLDs called *macro cells*. The more flexible interconnection network allows for a better utilization of the logic resources when compared to an SPLD. Figure 2.1(b) shows the architecture of a Xilinx CoolRunner-II CPLD as an example.

2.1.2 FPGAs

Field-programmable gate arrays share common characteristics of two other architectural families. They consist of an uncommitted array of logic resources

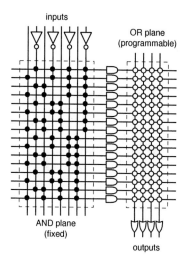

(a) SPLD

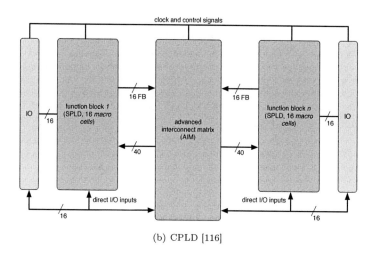

(b) CPLD [116]

Figure 2.1: Programmable logic devices. (a) SPLDs consist of regular logic arrays, while (b) CPLDs have more complex function blocks with an advanced interconnect network.

13

2 Background and Related Work

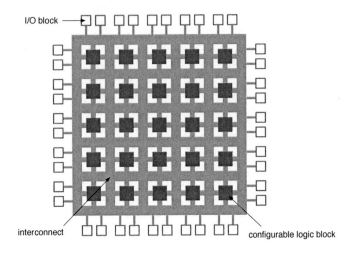

I/O block

interconnect   configurable logic block

Figure 2.2: Symmetrical FPGA architecture [25]. Configurable logic blocks and input/output blocks are joined by a programmable interconnection network.

like a mask-programmable gate array (MPGA), but are reprogrammable in both logic function and interconnect, much like a CPLD. The predominant type of *symmetrical* FPGAs, the architecture of which is depicted in Figure 2.2, was introduced in the 1980s by Xilinx, Inc., and consists of a regular array of *configurable logic blocks* (CLBs), which are connected by a similarly regular interconnection network. As opposed to CPLDs, the logic blocks are not custom-wired logic planes. Instead, as shown in Figure 2.3, they consist of *slices* containing look-up tables (LUTs), registers or flip-flops (FFs), and a collection of multiplexers (MUXs), allowing for flexible implementation of logic functions within the FPGA fabric, often distributed across several slices or CLBs.

The routing resources, which take up the large majority of a modern FPGA's physical die area [36], are divided into segments of varying lengths, providing local connections between adjacent cells as well as long-line resources that span larger parts of the device. The composition of the routing network significantly influences the overall efficiency of the implemented design.

In addition to logic resources and interconnects, modern FPGAs feature a set of dedicated elements for improving the performance and area efficiency of the implemented circuits:

14

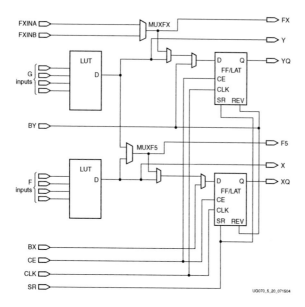

Figure 2.3: Logic slice of a Virtex-4 FPGA [118]. Two LUTs and two FFs are connected through a network of multiplexers (MUX).

Carry chains: For the implementation of fast arithmetic circuits, vertically adjacent slices are connected via communication lines dedicated to fast carry bit propagation. In some cases, these carry chains can also be used for implementing wide logic gates with minimal resources.

Input/output blocks (IOBs): The external pins of the FPGAs are mapped to regularly distributed IOBs, which also contain dedicated logic for matching the physical constraints of a wide set of IO interface standards. Modern FPGA families also include specialized high-speed interfaces for serial communication protocols.

Dedicated multipliers: To speed up certain arithmetic functions often found in signal processing applications, many FPGAs provide dedicated multiplier blocks, which permit higher operating frequencies and occupy less area than equivalent circuitry mapped to the logic blocks of the device. In some FPGA families, these blocks also support DSP-like operations such as multiply-and-accumulate (MAC).

Global clock distribution networks: Highly regular interconnection networks—driven by user-accessible clock buffers—allow a low-skew distribution of custom-generated clocks throughout the reconfigurable fabric. These networks are often segmented to provide power savings through selective clocking of individual parts of the device.

Additionally, there exist dedicated functional blocks for digital clock synthesis to enable clock frequency scaling and to improve the signal integrity of clocks used within the FPGA.

Memories: While the look-up tables of an FPGA's logic blocks can be used to implement memory elements, many designs feature dedicated synchronous memory blocks, which provide a higher density and performance. Distributed about the chip, these *Block RAMs* (BRAMs) can be used to implement read-only memories (ROMs), random-access memories (RAMs), and also more complex storage architectures such as FIFOs and content-addressable memories (CAMs).

Processors: Following the trend toward system-level integration on a single chip, many logic designs implemented within an FPGA include a microprocessor for software-based computations. While it is possible (and commonly implemented) to use the regular logic resources for the processor's implementation, select device families provide a dedicated processor core as a specialized block within the FPGA. Typically, such a hard-IP processor significantly exceeds the complexity and performance of fabric-implementable soft-core CPUs.

With rising densities and the inclusion of processors within the FPGA's fabric, many vendors label their top-of-the-line FPGAs as *platform FPGAs* to distinctively mark them as an implementation target for complex systems-on-chip (SoCs). They consequently provide different FPGA families featuring different amounts and subsets of the function blocks described above and target them at different markets. Figure 2.4 shows the floor plan of a Xilinx XC4VFX12 FPGA as an example of a platform FPGA and highlights the included dedicated function blocks within the reconfigurable fabric. It is these emerging *reconfigurable systems-on-chip* (rSoCs), also called *systems-on-programmable-chip* (SoPCs), that are the target of the programming model and execution environment discussed in this thesis.

2.1.3 FPGA Configuration

The *configuration* of an FPGA determines the content of the individual look-up tables and registers, the parameters of the different logic elements and other

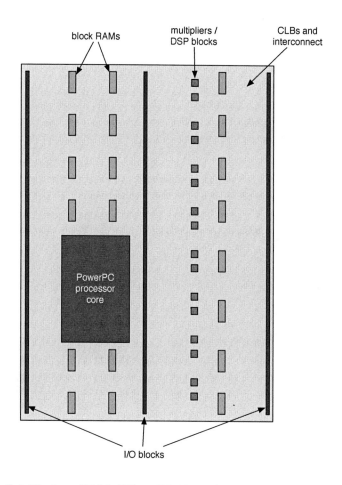

Figure 2.4: Platform FPGA (Xilinx XC4VFX12). Dedicated functional blocks like RAMs, multipliers, and a processor are embedded among the reconfigurable fabric (CLBs and interconnect).

modules, as well as the state of the switches controlling the interconnection networks. Programming an FPGA essentially means generating the configuration bitstream (see Section 2.2.3) and transferring it onto the device.

Configuration Storage

The configuration memory of commercially available FPGAs can be realized with either non-volatile or volatile storage elements. Non-volatile device types include anti-fuse FPGAs, where the configuration of the device is set by permanently disrupting or linking connections (fuses or anti-fuses, respectively) within the FPGA's fabric, and (E)EPROM or flash memory types, which store the configuration bitstream in reprogrammable, non-volatile memory elements. Volatile configuration storage is typically realized using SRAM memory. It has the advantage of short reconfiguration times, but comes at the cost of having to reload the configuration through an external interface on device power-up.

To this effect, vendors of SRAM-based FPGAs usually provide both memory interfaces and memory devices, so-called platform flash memories, for a straightforward set-up of a self-contained system. Similarly, it is possible to use the configuration interface of an FPGA to load its configuration through another external device, such as a microcontroller or a network interface.

Partial Reconfiguration

Most SRAM-based FPGAs on the market are only capable of a full system-level reconfiguration of the entire device, as shown in Figure 2.5(a). In this case, the device is reset and its configuration memory cleared before writing the new configuration. This also includes verification of the written bitstream on the device to detect transmission errors. After successful configuration, the device is reset again to ensure a defined initial state, the configuration bits are transferred from SRAM to the individual logic components, and the start-up sequence is initiated.

Several FPGA families are also able to perform a partial reconfiguration of only a subsection of its reconfigurable fabric using *partial bitstreams*, as shown in Figure 2.5(b). These devices are of particular interest to us, as they enable the dynamic exchanging of device functionality during run-time. In this case, the device is not reset prior to writing the partial bitstream, but all of the circuitry unaffected by the reconfiguration is kept operating. Through the use of an internal configuration access port (ICAP), some devices can perform a partial self-reconfiguration without involving an external controller. This ca-

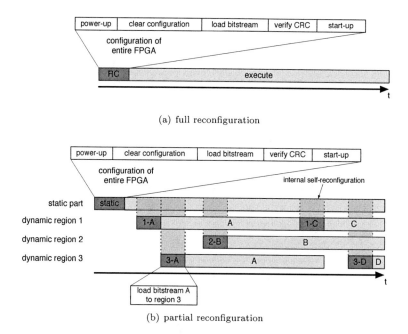

(a) full reconfiguration

(b) partial reconfiguration

Figure 2.5: Reconfiguration modes of Xilinx FPGAs. A full reconfiguration (a) resets and replaces the entire logic of the device, while a partial reconfiguration (b) can subsequently reconfigure only parts of the logic while the remaining circuitry keeps operating.

pability is a prerequisite for the mechanisms of hardware multitasking outlined in Chapter 6.

When preparing an FPGA design in order to be suitable for partial reconfiguration, the following design constraints must be observed:

Floor plan: The regions containing logic that will be reconfigured at run-time (the *dynamic regions*) must be strictly separated from the static portion of the design. This is achieved through area constraints observed by the design tools. While the interconnection resources of the dynamic regions can still be used for the routing of signals of the static region, the logic resources as well as any dedicated modules such as multipliers, memories, or processors are exclusive to the dynamic regions. Owing to the configuration infrastructure of the individual FPGAs, the placement of

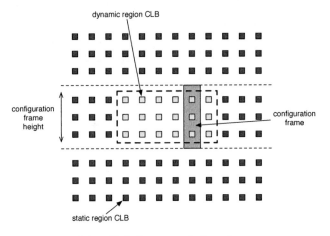

(a) multiple frames per device column

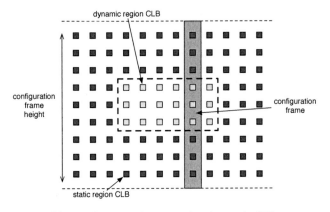

(b) reconfiguration frames overlapping static CLBs

Figure 2.6: Frame coverage for partial reconfiguration. Reconfiguration frames of recent devices (a) cover only parts of a device column, allowing for fine-grained reconfiguration. On older devices (b), other frames may be overwritten with their original content to achieve a similar effect.

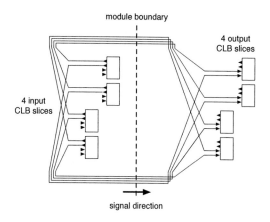

Figure 2.7: Basic 8-input, 8-output left-to-right bus macro [71].

dynamic regions must obey certain constraints. In early implementations of partially reconfigurable systems, a partial bitstream always reconfigured the complete height of the device, which rendered the IO blocks located above and beneath it unusable and gave rise to specialized one-dimensional (1D) reconfigurable platforms such as the XF-Board of the XFORCES project [108] and the Erlangen Slot Machine [73]. This restriction was due to the fact that the configuration bitstream is organized into frames, which, in older FPGA families, span the entire height of the device. Subsequent improvements in the design tools as well as changes in the configuration architecture of more modern FPGAs somewhat relaxed these constraints, enabling the use of two-dimensional (2D) reconfiguration techniques. On one hand, the frames of newer devices span only part of the FPGA's height and can be written without disturbing vertically adjacent logic outside of the frame's reach (see Figure 2.6(a)). On the other hand, current design tools also allow inter-frame reconfiguration, where the parts of a frame that correspond to a static region simply overwrite the already present and identical logic of the static region (see Figure 2.6(b)). This, however, precludes these parts of the FPGA from using look-up tables as memories or shift registers. It is up to the designer to ensure that the design meets these constraints.

Bus macros: Interface signals crossing the boundary between static and dynamic regions must be routed through special interfaces, so called *bus macros* [71], as shown in Figure 2.7. These can be placed anywhere on the boundaries of a dynamic region and ensure that the interface signals of different partial bitstreams line up with the static part of the design. Bus macros are specific to the employed FPGA family and exist in both asynchronous and synchronous variants. The latter route their signals through an additional register stage and help to avoid disrupting the timing behavior of the system through additional propagation delays.

Clock signals are an exception to this rule; they are always routed using dedicated clock distribution resources and do not require additional bus macros.

All devices available today that are capable of dynamic reconfiguration are SRAM-based FPGAs; thus, during the remainder of this thesis, we will only consider this type of field programmable gate arrays when referring to 'reconfigurable hardware, logic, or devices'.

2.2 Programming Models for FPGAs

Programming a reconfigurable logic device, such as an FPGA, is considerably different from programming a sequential microprocessor. Traditional FPGA design is for the most part a process of hardware development, and uses much the same design entry tools as, for example, a structured ASIC design. This fits well with the traditional application of FPGAs as prototyping platforms, but is also a fundamental cause for productivity and scalability issues when applied to modern high-density platform FPGAs and rSoC design principles.

2.2.1 Hardware Description Languages

The primary method for describing hardware to be mapped to an FPGA is a hardware description language (HDL) such as VHDL [69] or VeriLog [84]. Originally designed as a means for exact documentation of hardware components, HDLs have quickly gained tool support first for simulation and later for hardware synthesis.

The re-use of parts of a hardware description at a process level is often complicated by the numerous parallel interactions of the individual components. Also, HDL modules often feature highly specialized interfaces for a given design, also making direct re-use of their descriptions difficult. Thus, most vendors of intellectual property (IP) cores assure the interoperability of their modules either by providing them with fixed bus interfaces to standard buses, such as AMBA [68], Wishbone [85] or CoreConnect [54], or rely on an added layer for interface descriptions, which usually require a proprietary or standards-compliant tool chain (e.g., Xilinx EDK, IP-XACT [20]). Both methods, however, only specify the interactions on the very low level of module connections; most components still impose a specific transmission protocol on their communication partners, e.g., through a dedicated set of registers.

As a consequence, the scalable integration of hardware accelerators in a reconfigurable system-on-chip using HDL descriptions is an error-prone task with limited productivity. Although design turnaround times for reconfigurable hardware are significantly shorter than those for ASIC development, they still exceed the fast recompilation cycles known from pure software development by orders of magnitude. However, HDLs still hold the largest potential for exploiting the performance of fine-grained, parallel programmable logic.

2.2.2 High-Level Descriptions

To ease the task of hardware development and open the potential of FPGAs to software programmers, new high level language to gates (HLL-to-gates) translators have appeared as alternatives to working in an HDL [27, 46, 56, 81]. The majority of these efforts, with HandelC [27] and ImpulseC [56] as popular examples, try to provide a more C-like environment with abstract data types and familiar programming language syntax. The primary issues faced by these languages is how best to represent and exploit parallelism within an inherently sequential language, as well as how to handle the differences in data types, timing description and memory access between hardware and software descriptions. In particular, HDLs differ from sequential software languages in the following aspects:

Specialized data types: In addition to the 'regular' data types supported by most software languages, HDLs feature distinct hardware-oriented data types to model digital signals, or bits. These data types can model not only the binary values ('0', '1') of a bit, but also other states such as high-impedance ('Z'), unknown ('X'), weak, or strong.

Explicit timing description: Hardware description languages are able to express the explicit timing behavior of the described circuit by modeling clock transitions and events. A compiler for software languages must find a suitable schedule to guarantee correct execution of the sequential description.

Implicit parallelism: The structural elements of a hardware description (*modules* and *processes*) represent individual parts of the system that generally operate simultaneously. Sequential operation must be explicitly modeled using synchronizing signals. On the other hand, identifying and exploiting parallelism within a sequential software language is difficult [41]. Optimizing compilers for augmented C languages employ techniques for unrolling loops to expose implicit parallelism when creating the accelerator. Additionally, most languages provide new constructs to be used by the designer to explicitly identify parallelism.

Explicit memory access: While software languages handle memory transfers implicitly, in a hardware description, memories are modeled as distinct blocks with dedicated interfaces which must be explicitly instantiated and communicated with.

Similarly, the mapping from domain-specific languages to FPGAs is an active research topic [66, 91], and vendors of domain-specific modeling tools have begun to augment their collection of code generators for embedded microcontrollers with new tools targeting programmable logic devices [105, 119]. This enables the modeling and simulation of a high-level description within an established and familiar environment, while at the same time offering programmable logic as a high-performance execution environment.

The majority of high-level design tools for programmable logic produces a standard HDL description as an intermediate step to be processed by the regular FPGA design flow, as outlined in the next section.

2.2.3 FPGA Design Flow

The design flow from an HDL description of an FPGA design to the final bitstream involves the following steps:

Synthesis: In this step, the synthesis tool tries to derive an implementation of the logic described in the input description in terms of digital logic components at the register-transfer level (RTL). For example, synchronous signal assignments are turned into register instantiations and boolean operators are translated into logic gates. This step also involves optimizations of the synthesized design, such as logic minimization.

Technology Mapping: After synthesis, the RTL components are mapped to the physical components actually present in the hardware architecture. For instance, registers are mapped to slice flip-flops, and logic gates are translated into look-up table contents. During this step, additional optimizations of the logic are performed. The resulting netlist is already specific to the targeted technology (i.e., FPGA device family).

Placement: In the next step, the logic components of the mapped netlist are placed onto the FPGA's fabric, using heuristics to optimize the design

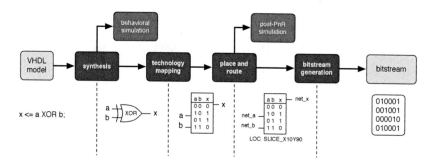

Figure 2.8: FPGA tool flow. A VHDL description is first *synthesized* in to a netlist, which is then *technology-mapped* and *placed and routed* for a target device before creating the final *bitstream*. Simulation of varying detail is possible at different stages (e.g., after synthesis or place-and-route).

for latency. This step can be performed iteratively with the routing step to obtain better results.

Routing: During the routing phase, the placed components from the previous step are connected using the FPGA's interconnection resources.

Bitstream generation: In the final step, the placed and routed design is turned into a bitstream file containing the configuration commands and data for the target device.

Figure 2.8 gives an overview of the entire process with an example of synthesizing, mapping, placing and routing a combinational function. Most available tool flows also allow the creation of simulation models at individual stages of the flow to evaluate the system at various levels of abstraction detail.

2.2.4 rSoC Tool Flow

Going with the trend toward platform FPGAs, many vendors provide tools for assembling reconfigurable system-on-chip comprising processors, bus topologies, peripheral cores, and memories from a high-level platform description. Using these tools, the designer specifies the IP components, interconnections, bus addresses, and other parameters of the final design without writing any code in a low-level hardware description language. As an example, the tool provided by Xilinx is called the *Embedded Development Kit* (EDK), while Al-

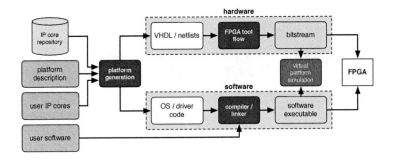

Figure 2.9: rSoC tool flow. Hardware and software architectures are generated from a unified platform description. Dark boxes designate the flow's processes.

tera calls its equivalent software *SoPCBuilder*. Often, these tools include (or are integrated with) development environments for designing the associated software to be run on the embedded processors.

For a higher level of customizability, it is possible to create custom IP components to be integrated in these environments. This applies not only to custom bus-attached peripherals, but to any conceivable hardware core implementable on the target FPGA.

Figure 2.9 outlines the assembly process of a system-on-chip using the Xilinx EDK. The initial description consists of two architecture files describing the composition of the system with its associated parameters, one for the hardware and one for the software part. Starting with this description, the IP cores are synthesized and integrated in a single, top-level VHDL description, which is then processed using the standard tool flow for FPGAs as described above. The software is granted considerably more flexibility and is usually compiled and linked by the user; here, the platform description's parameters are typically integrated using header files and preprocessor directives.

2.3 Operating Systems and Reconfigurable Hardware

In the last decade, operating systems for reconfigurable computers have been researched from a number of different angles. Early work on concepts and functions for such operating systems was quickly followed by efforts toward integrating reconfigurable hardware circuits as tasks into main-stream operating systems. In this section, we review recent related work and discuss its impact on and relation to this thesis' contributions.

Brebner [23, 24] was one of the first to discuss hardware multitasking. He proposed so-called swappable logic units that can be swapped in and out of a partially reconfigurable device, driven by an operating system. Other authors discussed further operating system functionalities. For example, Burns et al. [26] described operating system functions that perform translation and rotation operations on hardware circuits to better fit them to the device. Merino et al. [76] split the reconfigurable surface into so-called slots and used the operating system to schedule hardware tasks to these slots. Shirazi et al. [96] structured the runtime system into a monitor, a loader, and a configuration store and investigated trade-offs between reconfiguration time and circuit quality. Wigley and Kearney [110] made the case for including partitioning and allocation of reconfigurable resources as well as routing of hardware tasks as operating system functions.

In the following years, a large body of work has been focusing on single functions of future hardware operating systems. A prominent example is placement and scheduling of hardware tasks which has been studied under a variety of task and resource models as well as optimization objectives. Examples can be found in Jean et al. [57], Bazargan et al. [18], Teich et al. [104], Steiger et al. [102], Danne and Platzner [35], Danne et al. [33], and Pellizzoni and Caccamo [87]. Many efficient scheduling techniques, especially for real-time systems, rely on task preemption. The preemption of hardware is a challenging problem and has been studied and prototyped, e.g., by Simmler et al. [97] or Kalte and Porrmann [59]. Another issue related to placement and scheduling is the fragmentation of the reconfigurable logic area. While many of the presented placement and scheduling approaches try to avoid too much fragmentation, some authors proposed to compact the reconfigurable area from time to time. Examples can be found in Diessel et al. [37] and Compton et al. [29]. Most of these works were either theoretical or, if experimental, evaluated their algorithms by simulation studies on synthetic workloads, given the absence of available hardware operating system implementations and accepted benchmarks.

A number of prototypes have been created to demonstrate the feasibility of reconfigurable hardware operating systems. For instance, a networked reconfigurable platform for multimedia appliances that enables multitasking in hardware and software was shown by Mignolet et al. [78] and Nollet et al. [83]. Prototype creation has always been hindered by limitations of available technology and design tools. More importantly, all presented approaches viewed hardware tasks as coprocessors rather than *independent execution units*. A first step toward an approach that integrates hardware tasks as independent units was shown by Walder and Platzner [109] and Steiger et al. [102], respectively. In their prototype, hardware tasks have a higher degree of autonomy and can access operating system objects such as FIFOs, memory blocks, and I/O drivers and signal events to the operating system in order to drive the scheduler.

More recently, extensions of Linux have emerged that promote an OS-controlled integration of software and hardware processes. Kosciuszkiewic et al. [65] built on top of an existing Linux operating system kernel and viewed hardware tasks as a drop-in replacement for software tasks. These hardware tasks were executed on synthesized PicoBlaze soft-core processors and did not exploit the fine-grained parallelism provided by FPGAs. In the described implementation, the interaction between software threads and hardware tasks was limited to FIFO communication. Xie et al. [114] presented a similar heterogeneous multiprocessor system consisting of soft processor cores synthesized to an FPGA. Again, the Linux integration was limited to FIFO communication. Bergmann et al. [19] encapsulated access to hardware modules into software wrappers, the so-called *ghost processes* which provide a transparent interface for interactions from the kernel and other processes. The authors considered sharing the same address space between hardware and software execution units as unsuitable. Technically, they used *processes* instead of *threads* to encapsulate hardware modules. For communication between software and hardware, FIFOs mapped to the Linux file system as well as dual-ported memory accessible from both software processes and a hardware process were used, as shown by Williams et al. [112]. So et al. [99] also modified and extended a standard Linux kernel with a hardware interface, providing conventional UNIX inter-process communication (IPC) mechanisms to the hardware using a message passing network. Again, communication between hardware and software processes was implemented by FIFOs and mapped to file system-based operating system objects.

All these approaches tried to connect circuits implemented in reconfigurable hardware to existing operating system objects to ease communication between software and hardware. While simplifying the design of hardware/software systems to a certain degree, such an approach poses severe restrictions to the thread designer as only one specific communication service is available. In contrast, we believe that supporting a unified programming model for both software and hardware threads alike, supported by a rich set of operating system functions, is essential for exploiting the full potential of hybrid reconfigurable hardware/software systems while maintaining portability across different operating systems and hardware platforms.

A more closely related effort to our work is the *hthreads* project [86]. In hthreads, hardware threads are also managed by the operating system and are able to access various OS functions through a dedicated hardware thread interface, while sharing memory through a sophisticated inter-thread memory model [17]. hthreads is based on the POSIX pthreads programming model for both hardware and software threads and implements the OS components managing synchronization and task scheduling as hardware IP cores. In comparison to the approach presented in this thesis, hthreads sacrifices the flexibility of a software operating system kernel for exceptionally low response time and jitter [16], which caters to the needs of the targeted real-time embedded systems domain. hthreads also places a greater emphasis on heterogeneous multicore systems that integrate multiple microprocessors executing software threads. Our work, on the other hand, focuses on providing convenient hardware API support and integration of partial reconfigurability for hardware threads.

2.4 Chapter Conclusion

This chapter has established the background and related work for this thesis. We have introduced the relevant classes of reconfigurable logic devices and discussed the prevalent programming models and tool flows for FPGAs and reconfigurable systems-on-chip.

Related work on operating system approaches has been reviewed in Section 2.3. We have found that existing approaches to integrating reconfigurable logic into operating systems either focus on managing fundamental tasks for partial reconfiguration, such as fragmentation or module relocation, or still handle hardware modules as passive coprocessors. A common programming model integrating both software and reconfigurable hardware components under operating system control is so far missing within existing design approaches.

Based on this background, the next chapter will introduce the fundamental concepts of our multithreaded approach and outline the design objectives of the associated programming and execution environment.

CHAPTER 3

Concepts and Key Ideas

This chapter outlines the underlying concepts of our proposed multithreaded programming and execution models for reconfigurable hardware.

Reconfigurable hardware devices have evolved from small logic-centric chips to powerful hybrid platforms combining microprocessor cores with dense logic fabrics. Accordingly, the application domains for such devices have been extended from the original glue logic over prototyping and ASIC replacement to modern reconfigurable computers which allow for the mapping of both complex control-dominated tasks and data-centric parallel processing tasks to the same device. However, design methodologies for such configurable systems on chip have not kept up with the rise in complexity of reconfigurable hardware. In particular, there is little overlap between programming models and practices for embedded software and digital logic.

Multithreading, as pervasively employed in software-based systems, provides a flexible abstraction for grouping the functionalities of an application into threads and connecting them through suitable abstractions for communication and synchronization. We argue that this abstraction can be extended to reconfigurable computing systems, providing a common programming model for both hardware and software.

In the domain of software-based systems, the rising design complexity of evolving computing systems has been met by modular programming paradigms, standard libraries, and, eventually, operating systems. The driving idea behind an operating system is to take functionality that is required by all modules of the system and group it in a central place. Moreover, modern operating systems often play an essential part in making certain programming models possible in the first place. Complex concurrent programming models, such as multithreading, rely on a runtime infrastructure that is mostly transparent to the programmer. Major elements of an operating system providing multithreading support are, among others, a scheduler and synchronization and communication primitives. Thus, a logical step toward our goal of extending the multithreaded programming model to reconfigurable hardware is the creation of an operating system for reconfigurable hardware, which we call *ReconOS*.

Section 3.1 outlines the requirements and design goals of a programming model and operating system for reconfigurable hardware, which partially overlap with those for conventional operating systems. Section 3.2 introduces the multithreaded programming model and its components, as used and implemented by ReconOS. Finally, Section 3.3 gives a general overview of the fundamental hardware and software architecture; a detailed description of the actual implementation of the architecture is deferred to later chapters.

3.1 Design Objectives

Providing a unified multithreading programming model to both hardware and software components of a system enables significant improvements in productivity and ease-of-use when designing reconfigurable HW/SW systems. In order to let a system designer using our multithreaded operating system benefit from these advantages, we have defined the following design objectives regarding productivity, overheads, and adaptivity for ReconOS. The productivity gains are mainly influenced by the API and modeling environment presented to the user. The adaptivity goals, on the other hand, relate to the exploitation of the target device's partial reconfiguration capabilities as supported by the programming model and the run-time system.

3.1.1 Productivity

As the current design methodologies for hybrid reconfigurable systems-on-chip are mostly lacking in areas relating to design productivity, most of our design objectives focus on advances in this area. In particular, ReconOS intends to simplify the hardware/software partitioning of a system, increase portability of hardware modules, and support the re-use of existing and separately designed hardware and software components.

Hardware/Software Partitioning. When distributing the components of an application across a hybrid CPU/FPGA system, the optimal HW/SW partitioning is not always obvious from the beginning. Using traditional design techniques, where the individual parts of an application may not be clearly separated and may not have well defined interfaces, migrating a component from hardware to software at a late stage of the development process involves major changes in other related components, and may even necessitate a major redesign of the system's architecture.

Using the same programming model for both hardware and software components is intended to simplify changes in the hardware/software partitioning, as threads can be seamlessly migrated from software to hardware at design time just by instantiating the appropriate hardware or software thread, respectively. In fact, the decomposition of a hybrid system into threads should allow for an incremental development style, in which initially all threads are prototyped in software—possibly on a development system using a standard threading API— and later refined by selecting threads amenable to parallelization and moving them into hardware. Because all threads use the same primitives for communication and synchronization, no changes to the systems other than the specific thread creation calls are necessary.

The incremental refinement process and the resulting performance increases are detailed in Section 5.2 and demonstrated by the case study in Section 7.3.1.

Portability. A programming model should specify only the policies with which parts of an application interact, but should not significantly constrain the mechanisms with which the underlying run-time environment is implemented. Consequently, a hybrid HW/SW application written using our proposed multithreaded model should be portable across different platforms, both in terms of the employed host operating system, as well as the targeted processor architecture. By leveraging existing implementations of our programming model's primitives present in popular software operating systems, and by providing a unified interface for hardware threads across different platforms, we intend to provide a suitably portable programming model.

Section 7.3.2 shows an example of the portability of ReconOS' programming model and execution environment.

Legacy Components. For modern software systems a multitude of established software solutions exists for a variety of application areas, ranging from standard networking stacks through cryptography functions to video processing frameworks. A development environment for embedded systems should not impose any restrictions on the use of these legacy software components but enable their integration in a straightforward and familiar way. Similarly, it should enable existing hardware IP components with their specialized interfaces to be easily integrated into the programming model used by the larger system.

An example of the integration of existing software libraries is given by two case studies incorporating TCP/IP networking as described in Sections 7.3.1 and 7.3.3.

3.1.2 Low Overheads

The main reason for introducing dedicated hardware into an embedded system is usually the expectation of increased application performance. Although the abstractions provided by the multithreaded programming model will undoubtedly introduce a certain overhead, an application designer will expect operating system support in optimizing his application for increased performance.

While the individual performance of an application on a hybrid HW/SW system almost exclusively depends on the implementation and partitioning of the respective components and their use of the parallelization techniques offered by the platform (see Section 4.2), the design of our proposed operating system can provide means to increase the efficiency of the system by keeping the system calls' overheads low and by exploiting the partial reconfiguration capabilities of the employed FPGAs.

A quantitative evaluation of the timing and reconfiguration overheads can be found in Section 7.2.

3.1.3 Adaptivity

Applying the multithreaded programming model provides a modularization well suited to supporting the partial reconfiguration capabilities of platform FPGAs. Integrating the necessary reconfiguration management and infrastructure components within the operating system should substantially reduce the design complexity of partially reconfigurable systems.

ReconOS offers two modes of partial reconfiguration, which are transparently selected depending on the user's design of the hardware threads: explicit HW/SW repartitioning and transparent hardware multitasking.

Explicit HW/SW Repartitioning. The individual efficiency of a thread's hardware implementation may greatly depend on the current state of the system and/or the characteristics of the input data. It appears sensible to assume that different hardware/software partitionings may provide the best achievable performance at different points during an application's execution. Thus, the execution environment should allow the application to change the hardware/-software partitioning at run-time.

The case study in Section 7.3.3 underlines the feasibility of this approach.

Transparent Hardware Multitasking. Similar to the preemptive context switching capabilities of modern software operating system kernels, an operating system for reconfigurable hardware should be able to use the partial reconfiguration feature of its target platform to hide periods of a thread's inactivity— e.g., introduced by blocking functions—by transparently suspending such a thread, removing it from the reconfigurable fabric, and replacing it with another, runnable thread.

Chapter 6 details our approach to transparent hardware multitasking and its implementation.

3.2 Programming Model

In the embedded systems domain, real-time operating systems such as Vx-Works [113], RTXC [89], eCos [40], and many proprietary systems provide the designer with a set of clearly defined objects and associated services, which are encapsulated in application programmer interfaces, e.g., the POSIX API [55]. Among these basic objects, we typically find *threads* and *processes* as units of execution, *semaphores* and related services for synchronization, and *mailboxes* and their derivatives for communication. Threads are mostly characterized as light-weight processes featuring a fast context switch. While threads within a process share a common address space, different processes are isolated from each other. Real-time operating systems typically offer dynamic priority-based preemptive scheduling for threads, minimized interrupt latencies, bounded execution times for system calls, and are highly configurable to satisfy small memory footprint requirements.

The set of objects offered by an operating system together with the used scheduling policy can be understood as a programming model. While this model is not comparable to formal models of computation, it does provide a designer with an established way of structuring an application. Figure 3.1 sketches an example of an application composed of several threads, semaphores, message queues, and a shared memory region. In this example, THREAD_A reads

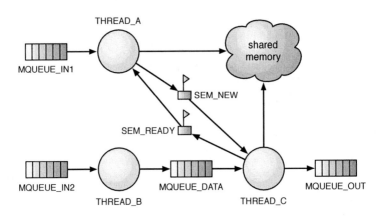

Figure 3.1: Example of a multithreaded application with three threads communicating using message queues and shared memory. Concurrent memory access is sequentialized using semaphores.

data out of a message queue, processes it, and writes the result to a shared memory region, synchronizing concurrent access to the shared memory with THREAD_C via two semaphores. When going from a CPU-based system to a CPU/FPGA platform, it seems natural to extend the services offered by the operating system to customized hardware cores. Analogous to a software thread, a hardware core performing a specific task can be thought of as a *hardware thread*.

In ReconOS, software and hardware threads integrate and communicate seamlessly and transparently with the operating system using the same set of operating system services. We argue that this approach to integrating hardware cores into a processor-based system greatly eases application development and significantly increases designer productivity.

ReconOS applications are typically crafted from the following operating system objects:

Threads are the basic units of *execution* which make up an application. It is up to the developer to partition an application into threads, which then communicate and synchronize using other operating system objects.

Semaphores and Mutexes provide a means for high-level *synchronization*. They can be used to sequentialize execution of threads, to protect critical code regions, or to manage exclusive access to shared resources.

Shared memory, message queues, and mailboxes are used for inter-thread *communication*. Generally, access to shared memory must be protected by synchronization primitives, as is necessary for any shared resource. Message queues and mailboxes occupy a special niche among the operating system objects – they provide both communication and synchronization at the same time.

The fact that all inter-thread activity is carried out using only these objects provides complete transparency within these interactions; a thread does not need to know whether its communication or synchronization partners are located in hardware or software—which in turn greatly facilitates design space exploration with respect to the hardware/software partitioning. Also, as long as the interfaces to the respective operating system objects are supported, the interoperability and portability of threads can be easily maintained when moving to a different target platform.

OS object	POSIX API [55]	eCos API [40]
Semaphores	`sem_post()` `sem_wait()`	`cyg_semaphore_post()` `cyg_semaphore_wait()`
Mutexes	`pthread_mutex_lock()` `pthread_mutex_unlock()`	`cyg_mutex_lock()` `cyg_mutex_unlock()`
Condition variables	`pthread_cond_wait()` `pthread_cond_signal()` `pthread_cond_broadcast()`	`cyg_cond_wait()` `cyg_cond_signal()` `cyg_cond_broadcast()`
Message queues / mail boxes	`mq_send()` `mq_receive()`	`cyg_mbox_post()` `cyg_mbox_get()`
Shared memory	$*ptr = value$ $value = *ptr$	
Threads	`pthread_exit()` `pthread_create()`	`cyg_thread_exit()` `cyg_thread_create()`

Table 3.1: Overview of software API functions.

Table 3.1 gives an overview of the most important operating system objects, and the respective API functions as provided by two representative software APIs: the POSIX standard and the eCos operating system kernel API. While different APIs and run-time environments generally provide similar services, their implementations sometimes vary: the message queue primitive provided by POSIX, for instance, supports messages of arbitrary lengths, whereas eCos' mailbox primitives are limited to single words of 32 bits. This must be taken into account when extending the model to hardware threads. It should be noted that it is the set of programming model primitives, not the individual API calls, that provides the mentioned benefits of the multithreaded programming model as implemented by ReconOS. For example, a software thread using the POSIX API can communicate seamlessly with a hardware thread using the ReconOS API (outlined in Section 4.3.2), as long as they use the same programming model abstraction (e.g., a mailbox/message queue).

Figure 3.2 shows the abstraction layer provided by ReconOS. The unified programming model allows the mapping of a multithreaded application onto both reconfigurable hardware—through hardware threads connected to a supporting infrastructure—or software—regular software threads executed on a microprocessor—, both controlled by a software host OS. The ReconOS API essentially provides POSIX-like functions as one single development model for both software and hardware execution contexts. ReconOS leverages standard operating system kernels for the implementation of operating system services. These operating systems also allow for running existing code and facilitate the access to a variety of I/O devices. This approach gives a designer the means to map an application to a portable model that can be directly executed on a wide range of CPU/FPGA execution platforms.

3.3 ReconOS Architecture

This section gives a brief overview about the most important architectural concepts of a ReconOS system. These concepts and their implementations form the basis of the ReconOS execution environment and will be discussed in more detail in the following chapters.

In ReconOS, the reconfigurable fabric is segmented into *slots* of arbitrary size, position, and shape, each of which represents the execution environment for one static (or several dynamically reconfigurable) hardware thread. A slot also establishes the necessary physical design entity for hardware multitasking by encapsulating regions for partial reconfiguration, as discussed in Chapter 6. Software threads, as well as the OS kernel, are executed on the embedded CPU. Instead of implementing the operating system functionality as defined by the programming model with dedicated hardware modules, ReconOS tries to re-use much of the functionality already provided by existing software operating system kernels, and makes it available to reconfigurable hardware. The layout of a typical ReconOS system with four slots is shown in Figure 3.3.

The design of ReconOS to support our programming model and its execution on hybrid CPU/FPGA platforms is distributed across a software architecture, which includes the necessary concepts and routines to map reconfigurable hardware threads into a software OS kernel, and a hardware architecture, which provides the physical partitioning, layout and infrastructure of hardware threads,

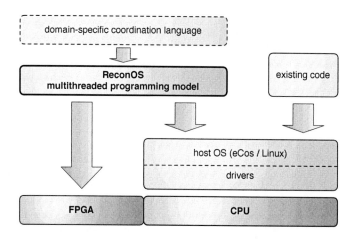

Figure 3.2: ReconOS abstraction layers. The programming model allows transparent interactions between elements mapped to the FPGA or executed on a CPU on top of an operating system.

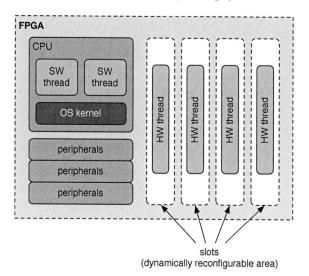

slots
(dynamically reconfigurable area)

Figure 3.3: A typical ReconOS system with four slots. Hardware threads are mapped within the slots in the FPGA's fabric, while software threads and the OS kernel are run on the system's CPU.

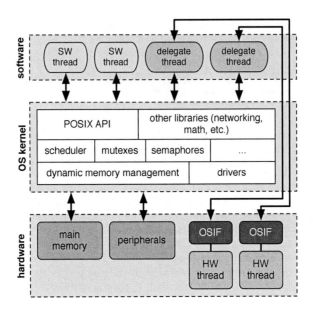

Figure 3.4: Conceptual overview of a ReconOS system. Software threads interact directly with the OS kernel, while hardware threads in the FPGA's logic fabric are connected through OSIF and delegate threads.

interface components, and interconnect topology. Figure 3.4 shows a conceptual view of a ReconOS system. Naturally, as our programing model spans across and blurs the hardware/software boundary, the hardware and software architectures of ReconOS blend into each other and share the implementation of important concepts, which set ReconOS apart from traditional rSoC design approaches:

- By augmenting **hardware threads** with a specially structured state machine description together with VHDL mappings for important OS calls, we allow hardware threads to autonomously interact with the operating system.

- The **operating system interface (OSIF)** is a dedicated hardware module that represents the connection between the software OS kernel and the hardware thread. It handles hardware thread OS calls as well as providing a communication interface for delegate threads (see below) running on the CPU.

- A **delegate thread** is a proxy software routine that retrieves OS call requests from the OSIF and executes them with the software OS kernel on behalf of a hardware thread.

- A **two-bus interconnect topology** ensures that OS control communication with low latencies and overheads is independent from high-throughput memory communication of the hardware threads.

- Exploiting **partial reconfiguration** requires both hardware support in terms of interface blocks and reconfiguration control and software support in terms of thread management and scheduling.

The implementations of all programming model objects are implemented within the OS kernel, together with related management services and drivers. Software threads rely on the standard API provided by the OS, whereas hardware threads are connected through their OSIF to a delegate software thread. Other hardware components are driven through the standard hardware abstraction layer of the operating system. Similar to a software-only operating system, the kernel is tasked with general management functions such as thread and memory management. We will show in subsequent chapters how some of these services need to be modified in order to support reconfigurable hardware threads.

3.3.1 Hardware Thread Design

To allow arbitrary hardware modules to be managed as autonomous threads within ReconOS, they need to be augmented with a specially structured finite state machine (FSM) description. In this state machine, VHDL procedures equivalent to software OS API calls can be used to interact with operating system objects such as semaphores, mutexes, or shared memory. Connected to an operating system interface, these VHDL procedures transparently initiate the communication process with the delegate thread (see below) and subsequently the operating system kernel. Together with the OSIF, this design approach allows fine-grained control over the hardware thread's execution while avoiding any unwanted interference with the parallel execution of the data paths of the hardware thread. A detailed description of the API and the FSM design process can be found in Section 4.3.2.

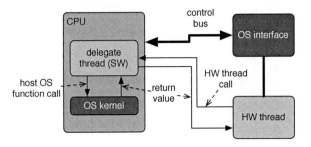

Figure 3.5: OS call relaying process. The hardware thread signals a pending OS request to its delegate, which retrieves and executes it before passing the return value back to the hardware thread.

3.3.2 Operating System Interface

The driving feature of the ReconOS approach is the fact that hardware threads can access the same programming model objects as their software counterparts. The implementation of these objects, such as semaphores or mutexes, is provided by the operating system kernel running on the CPU. The task of the operating system interface is to handle operating system calls from the hardware threads by either executing them directly, if they can be processed in hardware, or by relaying them to the CPU. At the same time, the OSIF also handles all control communication from the OS to the reconfigurable hardware, such as reset, state save/restore, or reconfiguration commands. A detailed description of the OSIF's features and mechanisms can be found in Section 4.4.

3.3.3 Delegate Threads

Once an OS request originating from a hardware thread has been relayed to the CPU, it needs to be translated into an actual software OS system call to the operating system kernel. To this end, ReconOS creates a separate software thread, the *delegate*, for every hardware thread. This delegate thread executes the operating system calls on behalf of its hardware thread and relays any return values back to the corresponding OSIF. Figure 3.5 illustrates the proxy-like relationship between a hardware thread and its delegate.

Although introducing measurable timing overheads through necessary interrupt processing and context switching on the CPU, this approach has three crucial advantages:

Transparency: For the kernel, operating system calls initiated in hardware cannot be distinguished from calls initiated by software threads, which provides the aforementioned transparency with respect to a thread's execution context (hardware or software).

Portability: Since a delegate thread is executed as a regular software thread (e.g., in user space, for systems that distinguish execution privileges for application and kernel code), no modifications to the operating system kernel apart from a generic OSIF driver are necessary. This makes the ReconOS approach easily adaptable to other operating systems. Section 5.1 provides examples of this.

Flexibility: Making additional OS calls available to hardware threads involves relatively small changes to the delegate thread, again without necessitating any changes to the kernel. The ReconOS tool chain simplifies this process by automatically generating the delegate thread code from a command definition provided at compile time (see Section 5.2.2).

A detailed description of a delegate thread's functionality can be found in Section 4.5.3. Additionally, Section 6.5 outlines delegate thread interactions with the scheduling subsystem for partially reconfigurable ReconOS systems, and Section 7.2.2 quantifies the involved overheads.

3.3.4 Two-Bus Interconnect

The ReconOS hardware architecture, shown in Figure 3.6, is oriented at a standard processor bus topology, as promoted by widely available SoC design tools, such as the Xilinx EDK (see Section 2.2.4). The basic system architecture is independent from the employed host operating system.

Hardware threads are connected to the system via their OS interfaces, which, in turn, are connected to the system's buses. ReconOS systems employ two separate buses: a memory bus and a control communication bus. The memory bus is used for high-throughput data transfers. Both the CPU cache subsystem and the hardware threads use it to access main memory and system peripherals. All control communication between the OS kernel on the CPU and the threads' OS interfaces is routed across a separate control bus. The separation of control and data communications provides several benefits:

Higher memory throughput: OS control communications do not obstruct data communications on the memory bus, thus reducing bus arbitration overhead and latency.

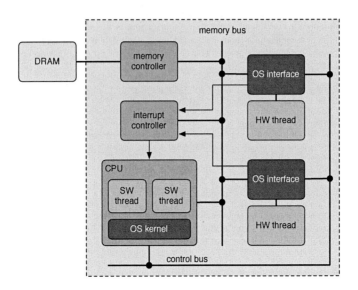

Figure 3.6: ReconOS hardware architecture. Hardware threads use their OSIF to access control and memory buses.

Lower OS call latency: Vice versa, memory communications, especially bursts, can not interfere with OS communications. This reduces jitter in the latency of OS calls, which increases the applicability of ReconOS in real-time environments.

Modular communication infrastructure: OS interfaces for hardware threads that do not need direct access to system memory can be synthesized without the memory interface, thereby greatly reducing the area footprint (see Section 7.2.1). Such threads are typical for many signal processing applications that arrange filter stages in pipeline form, connected by dedicated communication channels such as hardware FIFOs (see Section 4.4.4).

3.3.5 Partial Reconfiguration

The decomposition of an application into threads provides a suitable separation of modules for both parallel execution as well as for better resource utilization through multitasking, i.e., time-sharing of computational resources. In the case of reconfigurable hardware, multitasking is implemented through the use of partial reconfiguration, and managed by the operating system. The

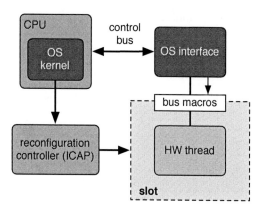

Figure 3.7: Partial reconfiguration architecture. A *slot* is controlled by a single OSIF and provides the execution environment for partially reconfigurable threads.

actual process of reconfiguration is transparent to the user and utilizes the structure established by the ReconOS hardware thread model. A ReconOS slot, as introduced above, provides the area in which hardware threads can be (re-)configured. Because every slot is connected to exactly one OSIF, there can be only one hardware thread in every slot at a given time. The necessary infrastructure for partial reconfiguration, as outlined in Section 2.1.3 and shown in Figure 3.7, is automatically added to every slot by the ReconOS tool chain. This includes bus macros for deterministic signal routing and control lines for selective disabling outgoing connections during reconfiguration, as well as a dedicated IP core for accessing the target device's ICAP.

A detailed description of the low-level mechanisms and architectural features implemented to facilitate partial reconfiguration of hardware threads can be found in Chapter 6.

3.4 Chapter Conclusion

In this chapter, we have outlined the design objectives of our proposed reconfigurable operating system ReconOS. Our design focuses on improving the design productivity and adaptivity of modern hybrid CPU/FPGA systems while maintaining acceptable overheads. We have presented the multithreaded programming model which provides a unified modeling approach for hardware and software components of an application. Abstracting the specifics of a hardware module's interface into interactions with high-level programming model objects significantly raises the potential for module reusability and portability. By leveraging existing software operating system kernels, our approach provides a flexible execution environment for both hardware and software components.

The following chapter will elaborate on the provided concepts of ReconOS and detail the design process for hardware threads and the mechanisms for their integration into multithreaded software.

CHAPTER 4

Designing and Executing Hardware Threads

This chapter details the ReconOS concept for designing and executing hardware accelerators as hardware threads. For simplicity reasons, it only deals with the programming and execution environment for the case of statically mapped hardware threads and skips over the mechanisms for partial reconfiguration. These are discussed thoroughly in Chapter 6.

Section 4.1 contrasts our approach with the conventional method of implementing slave coprocessors, as implemented in current state-of-the-art reconfigurable systems-on-chip (rSoCs). Section 4.2 outlines two ways of improving system performance through parallelization in a multithreaded reconfigurable system, operation- and thread-level parallelism, and gives examples of each method.

In the following, we explain in detail how hardware threads are designed, implemented and connected to the system, and how they integrate with the software operating system kernel. Section 4.3 details the necessary hardware layout of a hardware thread in order to interact with the operating system interface (OSIF). It summarizes the ReconOS hardware API and how computations are structured in a typical hardware thread, and demonstrates the shown methods with a representative example. Section 4.4 explains the details of the OSIF and how the low-level communication and synchronization protocol between a hardware thread and the operating system interface is implemented. Section 4.5 then takes the communication and synchronization a level higher and outlines the integration of hardware threads with multithreaded software.

4.1 Hardware Threads vs. Coprocessors

A commonly used model for connecting hardware accelerators realized in reconfigurable logic to a software-based system is that of the *slave coprocessor*. In this model, the custom logic module is typically connected to a central memory bus together with other peripherals like memory and I/O controllers, as shown in Figure 4.1(a). This also means that the most common mode of communicating with these hardware modules is through a highly accelerator-specific interface, such as a proprietary set of registers.

Slave coprocessors are the primary accelerator model supported by mainstream rSoC design entry tools (such as the Xilinx EDK or Altera's SoPCBuilder). These tools assist the developer by automatically instantiating necessary interface modules, assigning bus addresses and other connections, and providing reference templates or frameworks of modules with the desired interconnect to be fleshed out with the actual accelerator's functionality. This model is adopted by many reconfigurable systems-on-chip, and also appears to be a popular connection method in many research projects focusing on operating-system support for reconfigurable hardware [67, 107].

Bus interface	Slices	LUTs	FFs	Relative
PLBv34 (master/slave, 64-bit)[1]	1067 - 2593	1728 - 4546	1065 - 2211	2.4 - 5.9 %
PLBv34 (slave only, 64-bit)[1]	346 - 677	446 - 956	328 - 624	0.8 - 1.5 %
PLBv46 (master, 64-bit)[2]	67 - 308	8 - 505	112 - 177	0.2 - 0.7 %
PLBv46 (slave, 64-bit)[3]	59 - ∼ 265.5	52 - 383	191 - 357	0.4 - ∼ 1.7 %
OPB (slave, 32-bit)[1]	27 - 526	9 - 816	36 - 442	0.1 - 1.2 %

Table 4.1: Area overheads for common rSoC bus interfaces (depending on configuration, relative device utilization given in terms of slices).

Slave coprocessors enjoy mature design tool support and incur relatively little area overhead in terms of slices, LUTs, and FFs, as representatively shown by the different CoreConnect interfaces listed in Table 4.1. Depending on the configuration and capabilities of the respective bus attachment (and of course on the size of the target device), the logic requirements of individual interface range from a negligible amount to about 6 % of the available FPGA area. Often, master and slave functionality can be separated, allowing an even closer fitting to the requirements of the application, with master interfaces typically requiring more logic than simple slaves.

---

[1]overheads given for a Xilinx Virtex-II-Pro device (XC2VP100)

[2]overheads given for a Xilinx Virtex-4FX device (XC4VFX100)

[3]overheads given for a Xilinx Virtex-5FXT device (XC5VFX100T)

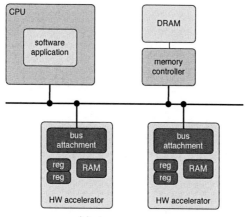

(a) slave coprocessor

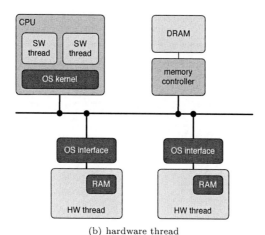

(b) hardware thread

Figure 4.1: Modeling hardware accelerators. Traditional approaches (a) regard hardware modules as passive slave coprocessors, while our approach (b) models them as autonomous hardware threads.

However, by employing these interfaces slave coprocessors are tied to a specific communication structure and protocol and require specific knowledge about the accelerator's hardware interface in order to develop software applications using it. On the hardware side, when creating a new accelerator, the developer must observe the specific tool and interconnect protocols and capabilities, and frequently has to spend considerable time to create and test custom logic—e.g., for memory access functions or interrupt logic—where the application requirements do not exactly match the capabilities of the automatically generated interface templates. In summary, these proprietary accelerator interfaces considerably impede reusability, portability, scaleability, and, as a consequence, design productivity.

In contrast, our approach abstracts the communication and synchronization interfaces away from implicitly mapped registers or direct memory access (DMA) channels toward a general and well-defined set of programming model objects such as message queues and mutexes, as provided by the multithreaded programming model introduced in Section 3.2. In this way, hardware accelerators evolve from slave coprocessors to OS call capable hardware threads on a level with other software threads present in the system. The resulting system layout is depicted in Figure 4.1(b). This abstraction provides a more unified view and use of a rSoC's resources, and threads can be easily ported and reused, thanks to the generalized interfaces. From the programming model's perspective, there is no difference between hardware and software threads, and consequently no explicit boundary between hardware and software, which simplifies development and partitioning of hybrid systems. Together with a multithreaded execution model, hardware threads also have the potential of improving the utilization of an rSoC's reconfigurable fabric through hardware multitasking, as discussed in Chapter 6.

4.2 Exploiting Parallelism

A hybrid hardware/software system such as ReconOS has the capabilities of accelerating application execution by means of two distinct, but complementary design approaches: operation- and thread-level parallelism. While operation-level parallelism exploits the fine-grained nature of reconfigurable logic, thread-level parallelism takes advantage of the more coarse-grained description of parallelism inherent in multithreaded application development.

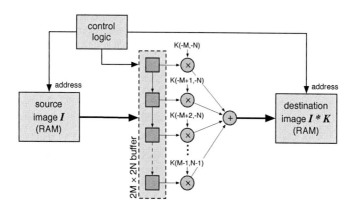

Figure 4.2: Hardware implementation of a convolution operator. The multiplications of the kernels elements with the image pixels can be computed in parallel.

4.2.1 Operation-Level Parallelism

In a sense, the logic contained in an FPGA's reconfigurable fabric offers a vast array of parallel processing resources. Given a suitable application (domain), FPGAs are often able to achieve significant speedups over general-purpose CPUs because of the fine-grained *operation-level parallelism* they can exploit. A prime example of an application domain amenable to this kind of parallelization is the area of image processing. Often, the same operation is performed for multiple regions of an image. An example of this is the the convolution operator $(*)$, which applies a convolution kernel K to an image I:

$$(I * K)(x, y) = \sum_{i=-M}^{M-1} \sum_{j=-N}^{N-1} I(x - i, y - j) K(i, j)$$

Because the resulting pixels of $(I * K)$ are independent of each other, they can be computed in parallel. A hardware implementation of a convolution is shown in Figure 4.2 and used in the application case study in Section 7.3.1. Similarly to the convolution operator, there exist many algorithms for which hardware implementations with significant speedups have been developed, such as, for example, Fast Fourier Transformations [121], linear algebra operations [122], or cryptography [77].

Other methods of exploiting the fine-grained and flexible nature of FPGAs are pipelining and specialized operators. Pipelining is essentially another method of parallel execution, where different computational stages of the pipeline are separated by storage elements and execute concurrently in a lock-step fashion. An example of specialized operators are bit-level manipulations or operations on binary values of large or non-standard widths, which can be mapped with substantially more efficiency to FPGAs than to general-purpose processors with fixed-width registers. Naturally, all these operation-level optimizations can be combined.

When decomposing an application into threads using the multithreaded programming model, those threads containing operations amenable to fine-grained parallelization are usually the best candidates for implementation as a hardware thread. Together with thread-level parallelization, as described in the next section, they provide the basis for the acceleration potential offered by ReconOS.

4.2.2 Thread-Level Parallelism

The concept of multithreading was originally developed to hide the latency of operations in a single processor by executing other independent tasks during these periods. This mechanism can be used both at a high level within an operating system's process scheduler, as well as on a lower, hardware-supported level within a CPU—which, of course, still requires software support. A prominent example is the hyper-threading or simultaneous multithreading (SMT) support in modern CPUs [31], in which the storage elements of the CPU are duplicated, allowing several concurrently executing threads to time-share the processor's functional units during blocking operations and presenting several virtual CPUs to the system. A more historic example are the ten virtual peripheral processors (PPs) of the Control Data Corporation's CDC 6600 series [106], which hides the I/O latencies of the main memory by executing other unrelated instructions (for other processes) while waiting for the memory access. Similar to SMT, the CDC 6600 provided ten PP register sets but only one instance of the actual processing hardware, and time-sliced program execution between the ten available threads. Also, many software applications are able to hide I/O latencies through multithreading, especially in server environments servicing multiple concurrent user requests, such as web or database servers.

Multithreading requires an application to be divided into concurrent threads of execution in order to provide independent executable code in the event of a blocking operation. This partitioning also lends itself to actual parallel execution on multiple independent processing elements, a property which we call *thread-level parallelism.* In the case of a larger ReconOS system that provides multiple slots for hardware threads, these slots can be seen as independent processors capable of executing several hardware threads in parallel. As long as the inter-thread data dependencies—as managed by the operating system through the provided programming model primitives—permit, such a system can improve overall processing performance by exploiting the thread-level parallelism of an application in hardware.

It should be noted that through partial reconfiguration of hardware threads, as discussed in Chapter 6, both thread-level parallelism as well as the hiding of I/O latencies can be combined.

4.3 Multithreaded Hardware/Software Development

In our proposed unified programming model, hardware and software threads use the same operating system services to communicate and synchronize, and consequently follow the same underlying structure regardless of their execution environment. As both kinds of threads are typically implemented in different languages—VHDL and C, respectively—that feature certain disparities (refer to Section 2.2.2, p. 23), we have supplemented the hardware design process with mechanisms further unifying the two development environments.

4.3.1 Software Threads

ReconOS software threads are identical to regular threads of the host operating system both in concept and implementation. Since software threads are handled by the standard OS scheduler, they are independent from the ReconOS extensions.

Software threads can be implemented using either the eCos kernel API or the POSIX pthreads API—the ReconOS operating system objects can be seamlessly mapped to either API. It is recommended to use POSIX where possible, as it is the more portable API of the two and is also supported via a compatibility layer in eCos. Listing 4.1 shows an example of a software thread implementing THREAD_A from the application introduced in Figure 3.1 (p. 36) using the POSIX API. Data is received from a message queue (MQUEUE_IN1, line 9), processed (line 10), and then copied to shared memory (line 12), which is synchronized using semaphores (SEM_READY, line 11, and SEM_NEW, line 13).

```
1    mqd_t mqueue_in1;
2    sem_t sem_new, sem_ready;
3    void *shared_mem;
4
5    void *thread_a_entry( void *data ) {
6        uint8 buf[ MSG_SIZE ];
7
8        while ( true ) {
9            mq_receive( mqueue_in1, buf, MSG_SIZE, 0 );
10           do_something( buf );
11           sem_wait( sem_ready );
12           memcpy( shared_mem, buf, MSG_SIZE );
13           sem_post( sem_new );
14       }
15   }
```

Listing 4.1: Code implementing software thread `THREAD_A`.

4.3.2 Hardware Threads

Software threads have sequential execution semantics. To use an operating system service, a software thread simply calls the corresponding function in the operating system library. Hardware threads, on the other hand, are inherently parallel. Mostly, there is no single control flow and, thus, no apparent notion of calling an operating system function. In particular, typical hardware description languages, such as VHDL, offer no built-in mechanism to implement *blocking calls*.

To present as unified a programming model as possible to the user, we rely on the following approach: We structure a hardware thread such that all interactions with the operating system are managed by a single sequential state machine. To this end, we have developed an operating system function library for VHDL. This library contains code implementing the system call signaling wrapped into VHDL procedures, e.g., `reconos_sem_wait()`. Together with the OSIF, a separate synchronizing logic module serving as the connection between the hardware thread and the OS, these procedures are able to establish the semantics of blocking calls in VHDL. A hardware thread thus consists of at least two VHDL processes: the synchronization state machine (FSM) and the actual user logic. The state transitions in the synchronization state machine always depend on control signals from the OSIF; only after a previous operating system call returns, the next state can be reached. Thus, the communication with the operating system is purely sequential, while the processing of the hardware

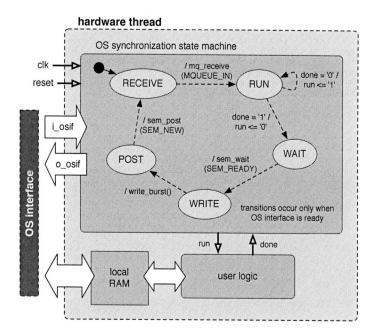

Figure 4.3: Example of an OS synchronization state machine. The state transitions are executed under OSIF control, allowing individual OS calls (e.g., `sem_wait()`) to block. The actual processing of the thread occurs in the user logic.

thread itself can be highly parallel. It is up to the programmer to decompose a hardware thread into a collection of user logic modules and one synchronization state machine. Besides the increased complexity due to the parallel nature of hardware, this process is no different from programming a software thread.

An example demonstrating this mechanism is depicted in Figure 4.3, which again represents `THREAD_A` from the example above. Listing 4.2 shows the corresponding VHDL implementation of the synchronization state machine, using ReconOS system calls. Analogous to the software thread in Listing 4.1, the hardware thread receives a message into the local RAM (lines 13ff.), processes it (lines 20ff.), waits for a semaphore (`SEM_READY`, lines 27ff.), writes the result to shared memory (lines 31ff.), and then posts another semaphore (`SEM_NEW`, lines 35ff.). The OS synchronization state machine and the user logic communicate via the two handshake signals *run* and *done*.

```
1   osif_fsm: process(clk, reset)
2     variable completed, success : boolean;
3   begin
4     if (reset = '1') then
5       state <= RECEIVE;
6       run <= '0';
7       reconos_reset(o_osif, i_osif);
8     elsif rising_edge(clk) then
9       reconos_begin(o_osif, i_osif);
10      if reconos_ready(i_osif) then
11        case state is
12
13          when RECEIVE =>
14            reconos_mq_receive(completed, success, o_osif, i_osif,
15                               MQUEUE_IN1, 0, MSG_SIZE);
16            if completed then
17              state <= RUN;
18            end if;
19
20          when RUN =>
21            run <= '1';
22            if done = '1' then
23              run <= '0';
24              state <= WAIT;
25            end if;
26
27          when WAIT =>
28            reconos_sem_wait(o_osif, i_osif, SEM_READY);
29            state <= WRITE;
30
31          when WRITE =>
32            reconos_write_burst(o_osif, i_osif, 0, SHARED_MEM);
33            state <= POST;
34
35          when POST =>
36            reconos_sem_post(o_osif, i_osif, SEM_NEW);
37            state <= RECEIVE;
38
39          when others => null;
40        end case;
41      end if;
42    end if;
43  end process;
```

Listing 4.2: Code for the example of Figure 4.3.

The FSM process resembles a regular VHDL state machine description, augmented with additional synchronization logic. This logic ensures that the state machine only transitions to the next state if the OSIF is ready. The corresponding VHDL procedures and functions, which need to be present in all ReconOS hardware threads, are `reconos_reset()` (line 7) for initializing the OSIF handshake lines, `reconos_begin()` (line 9) for setting the handshake lines to a default state prior to any OS call invocation, and `reconos_ready()` (line 10) for checking the OSIF ready signals. The OSIF ready signals reflect whether the software operating system is currently executing a—possibly blocking—system call on the hardware thread's behalf, effectively synchronizing the state machine with the OS call.

To further illustrate the underlying mechanism, consider the following sequence of events. Upon reaching the state *WAIT* in line 27, the procedure `reconos_sem_wait()` asserts the appropriate handshake signals in the OSIF to signal a ReconOS semaphore wait call. The *state* signal is set simultaneously to the next state, *WRITE*, in line 29. However, the OSIF immediately asserts a *blocking* signal, indicating that the request is being processed. On the next rising clock edge, the blocking signal, evaluated in `reconos_ready()` (line 10), prevents the synchronization state machine from entering the *WRITE* state. Only after the operating system call returns, the OSIF will deassert the blocking signal which allows the synchronization state machine to complete the state transition.

It should be noted that the local RAM is optional; single-word bus access is also possible through the OS interface. While inferior in performance to burst transactions, single-word accesses provide more flexible and convenient access for configuration data or for extracting single elements from complex data structures.

An overview of the operating system objects and their related ReconOS and POSIX API calls, as used by hardware and software threads, respectively, is shown in Table 4.2. Most hardware functions are direct counterparts to the POSIX software API. Notable exceptions include mailboxes, which provide separate sets of calls for blocking and non-blocking put and get operations, and memory accesses, which can explicitly request single-word or burst transfers. The ReconOS hardware API supports the most important subset of the calls available in POSIX; the incorporation of additional functions, such as calls for thread creation or scheduler control, requires only minimal extensions to the execution environment.

OS object	POSIX API (software)	ReconOS API (hardware)
Semaphores	`sem_post()` `sem_wait()`	`reconos_sem_post()` `reconos_sem_wait()`
Mutexes	`pthread_mutex_lock()` `pthread_mutex_unlock()`	`reconos_mutex_lock()` `reconos_mutex_unlock()`

Condition variables	`pthread_cond_wait()`
	 `pthread_cond_signal()`
	 `pthread_cond_broadcast()`
		`reconos_cond_wait()`
		 `reconos_cond_signal()`
		 `reconos_cond_broadcast()`

Message queues / mail boxes	`mq_send()`
	
	 `mq_receive()`
		`reconos_mq_send()`
		 `reconos_mbox_put()`
		 `reconos_mbox_tryput()`
		 `reconos_mq_receive()`
		 `reconos_mbox_get()`
		 `reconos_mbox_tryget()`

Shared memory	$*ptr = value$
	
	 $value = *ptr$
		`reconos_write()`
		 `reconos_write_burst()`
		 `reconos_read()`
		 `reconos_read_burst()`

Threads	`pthread_exit()`
	 `pthread_create()`
	 `pthread_delay()`
		`reconos_thread_exit()`
		 —
		 `reconos_thread_delay()`

Table 4.2: Overview of ReconOS API functions.

4.4 The Operating System Interface

The API provided by ReconOS makes the multithreaded programming model primitives available to hardware modules. The mechanisms defined in the previous section allow the invocation of the multithreaded API to be semantically as close to sequential software execution as possible. Such a design methodology enables the transparency and productivity gains referred to in Section 3.1. To provide a complete execution environment for hardware threads adhering to this development model, a system of several modules and mechanisms needs to be present for interfacing hardware threads to the operating system kernel.

This section details the necessary low-level protocol and its implementation for communication and synchronization between a hardware thread and its operating system interface (OSIF), as well as the mechanisms for executing certain operating system calls directly in hardware.

To be able to model hardware circuits executing on reconfigurable logic as threads, it is necessary to carefully define mechanisms for low-level synchronization and communication between the hardware circuitry and the operating system. In ReconOS, this is the task of the operating system interface. Figure

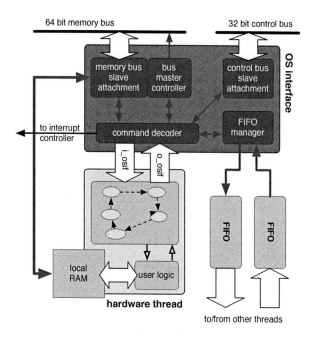

Figure 4.4: OSIF overview and interfaces. The command decoder manages all hardware thread interactions and relays data to the individual bus attachments, external FIFOs, or the CPU.

4.4 gives an overview of the OSIF's structure and its interfaces. On one side, the OSIF connects to the hardware thread's OS synchronization state machine and local RAM. On the other side, the OSIF provides interfaces to the system's memory and control bus. Further, the OSIF requires an interrupt line to the CPU's interrupt controller and features optional ports to connect to FIFO cores. The OSIF itself is built from several modules whose functions are described in the following.

4.4.1 Thread Supervision and Control

ReconOS provides hardware threads with a hardware API that comes in the form of a function library that specifies VHDL functions and procedures like `reconos_sem_post()` or `reconos_thread_exit()` (see Table 4.2). A designer

	Signal		Description
Thread	`command`	[0:7]	Requested OS call code
	`data`	[0:31]	OS call arguments
	`request`		Request strobe
	`error`		Error flag
OSIF	`data`	[0:31]	Return value of OS call
	`ack`		Acknowledges incoming request
	`step`	[0:3]	Current step of multi-cycle
	`valid`		Indicates success of call
	`busy`		System buses are busy
	`blocking`		Set while executing blocking OS calls

Table 4.3: OSIF communication protocol signals. The thread's signals are used to initiate OS calls or report errors, while the OSIF signals control the thread's FSM and transport return values. Numbers in parenthesis denote signal widths.

can use these procedures inside the thread's OS synchronization state machine to sequentially call operating system functions, much like a software thread uses functions from the operating system's C-API. As a consequence, every state of the OS synchronization state machine may contain at most one VHDL system call. The VHDL procedures are purely combinational and communicate with the OSIF through a set of incoming and outgoing signals, which are shown in Table 4.3.

The mechanisms that govern the OS call request-response interactions between the OSIF and the hardware thread are controlled by the *command decoder* module. This module receives OS call requests from the hardware thread, decodes them and initiates the appropriate processes to fulfill that request. This may involve, for example, raising an interrupt with the system CPU, initiating a bus master transfer or feeding data into a FIFO.

Since the operating system executing on the CPU cannot process OS calls within one clock cycle, the OSIF needs a means to suspend state transitions of the thread's OS synchronization state machine. This is achieved by having the OS synchronization state machine routinely check input signals from the OSIF before setting its next state (see `reconos_ready()` in Listing 4.2, line 10). This way, the OSIF can block the part of the hardware thread that interacts with the operating system, which effectively implements the semantics of blocking calls in VHDL.

The OSIF distinguishes between two conditions that can suspend state transitions: *busy* and *blocking*. The hardware thread is held in the *busy* state as long as there are pending bus transfers as a result of a thread's request. On the other hand, a thread enters the *blocked* state after calling an OS function that can lead to blocking on an OS resource, for instance `reconos_sem_wait()`. For the hardware thread, this distinction is arbitrary. The OSIF, however, manages blocking and busy internally in different ways. The *blocking* signal is a settable and resettable register that is indirectly controlled by the CPU, while the *busy* signal is set asynchronously by the memory and control bus modules.

Some of the supported OS calls require more than one 32 bit data argument. An example of such a call is a single-word memory access (`reconos_write()`), which needs both an address and a data argument. Other calls produce a return value, which the hardware thread needs to wait for (e.g., `reconos_mbox_get()`). Neither of these calls can be completed in a single clock cycle. Furthermore, these calls need to interact with the OSIF across multiple clock cycles, which rules out simply delaying the state transition until the call completes and then resuming with the next call.

To address these issues, the command decoder implements a mechanism for *multi-cycle commands*. In the case of a single call requiring different actions in subsequent clock cycles, the FSM state's VHDL procedure is evaluated for more than one clock cycle, and only if all steps are completed successfully, the OS synchronization state machine transitions to the next state. Every multi-cycle VHDL API procedure takes one additional argument, `completed`. This argument, implemented as a VHDL variable, returns *false* as long as not all steps have been completed. Only in the last step, `completed` is set to *true*, which then prompts the state transition. Thus, a multi-cycle command induces additional state which keeps track of the currently executing step of the command. This state is kept by the OSIF and transmitted via the `step` signal to the VHDL procedure, which uses it to perform the appropriate function for this step.

An example of this mechanism is depicted in Figure 4.5. Here, an OS call taking two arguments and returning a third value is requested, requiring three steps to complete. On entering state B of the OS synchronization state machine, the hardware thread invokes the appropriate VHDL procedure, which transmits the first (state B, step 0) and second (state B, step 1) argument. The OSIF then blocks the thread's OS synchronization state machine by setting the busy and/or blocking signals and relays the OS call to the CPU, where the associated delegate thread executes it. Upon returning from the software OS call, the OSIF unblocks the hardware thread and passes the return value in state B, step 2, where it is stored by the same VHDL procedure that invoked the call. Since step 2 is the last step of this command, the `completed` variable is set, prompting the OS synchronization state machine to enter state C, step 0 in the next clock cycle.

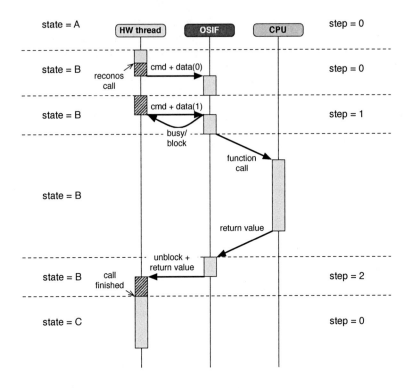

Figure 4.5: Example of a multi-cycle command. The command is evaluated in several iterations (steps) of a thread's FSM state, allowing multiple parameters and return values to be transferred.

This mechanism is highly flexible and largely transparent to the thread developer. It does, however, require some additional VHDL code to check for the `completed` variable (as shown in Listing 4.2, line 16).

4.4.2 Thread Initialization

In the established APIs, threads are usually passed an initialization argument upon creation. A software thread's entry function receives this value—which is often a pointer to a more complex user-defined data structure—via function call parameters placed on the stack. A hardware thread needs to call a dedicated `reconos_get_init_data()` API function to retrieve this value from its OSIF, and, in the case of a pointer to a memory data structure, can subsequently use memory access functions to read the required values from the system's main memory.

4.4.3 OS Call Relaying

OS services that are not provided by the OSIF directly (such as memory or FIFO access) are relayed to the OS kernel running on the CPU. Once the command decoder receives such a request from the hardware thread, it places the command and associated arguments in software-accessible registers on the control bus, and raises an interrupt with the CPU. This interrupt is forwarded to the software delegate thread associated with the hardware thread (see Section 4.5.3), which retrieves the command and arguments from the registers and executes the software OS call on behalf of the hardware thread. Any return values are placed in the OSIF's control bus registers, which pass the values on to the hardware thread.

This mechanism provides maximum flexibility, since virtually every call that is possible from a software thread can now be requested by a hardware thread as well. However, OS call relaying comes with a noticeable overhead which is quantified in Section 7.2.2. On every relayed OS call, the CPU needs to process an interrupt, switch to the associated delegate's context, and access the control bus registers before actually executing the call. During this time, the hardware thread's OS synchronization state machine remains suspended. This overhead is acceptable for synchronization operations, which cannot be handled outside of the kernel, and low-bandwidth communication, e.g., for control messages or data-augmented synchronization primitives, such as mailboxes. High-bandwidth communication, however, should be handled using programming model primitives which utilize the OSIF's hardware facilities for high-bandwidth communication, as discussed in the next section.

4.4.4 Data Communication Routing

Due to the substantial overhead involved in relaying OS requests to software, all high-throughput data communications should be handled in hardware without involving the CPU. The ReconOS OSIF features hardware support for several different communication primitives that provides the basis for any efficient, high-bandwidth thread-to-thread communication.

Memory Access

The memory bus attachment logic encapsulates the logic for direct memory access to the system's entire physical address space. Using the OSIF's capabilities, an attached hardware thread can access shared memory by means of convenient single word access or high-throughput burst transfers, both for read and write operations.

Single-Word Memory Access. By utilizing the OSIF's memory bus interface, a hardware thread has direct access to any memory location and bus-connected peripheral in the system. Single-word memory transfers can be serviced directly through the OS call (`reconos_read()` or `reconos_write()`) from within the OS synchronization state machine. This method is mainly provided for convenience, and its primary use is for retrieving thread parameters from shared data structures during initialization.

Burst Memory Access. Using the bus master controller (see Figure 4.4), it is also possible to transfer bursts of data to and from memory. To request a burst write, the hardware thread must first store the data to transfer in the thread-local RAM. Then, the thread's OS synchronization state machine calls a `reconos_write_burst()` procedure. This prompts the bus master controller to initiate a memory bus transfer of the requested size from the local RAM, which is mapped into the system memory space, to the target address in main memory. Similarly, a thread can request a burst read transaction, which will place data from main memory in the local RAM.

Caching Issues. Many embedded processors, such as the PowerPC 405 core included in certain Xilinx FPGAs and primarily used by ReconOS, feature a cache unit in the data path between CPU and the memory bus. Sharing a memory region between software threads running on this CPU and hardware threads directly connected to the memory bus requires the application designer to explicitly manage cache coherency issues, for example by manually flushing or invalidating cache lines before or after a synchronized data transfer between the threads. Most operating systems provide access to the processor's caches through simple cache-management functions within the host operating system's software API (e.g., in eCos), or more involved techniques integrated into the operating system's memory management (e.g., Linux' cache flush architecture). Although this somewhat dilutes the transparency of the programming model, there is no alternative to it on a platform without hardware support for cache coherency.

Virtual Memory. Depending on the capabilities and requirements of the host operating system (see Section 4.5), memory access from hardware threads must deal with an additional layer of complication: virtual memory. In such a system, user threads operate on virtual memory addresses that are transparently mapped to the corresponding physical memory locations.

As the OSIF is connected directly to the memory bus of the system, it can by default only deal with physical addresses. In the case of host operating systems that—for simplicity and performance reasons—do not provide virtual memory (such as eCos), this allows for simple sharing of physical memory addresses between software and hardware threads. However, as soon as the host operating system utilizes the CPU's memory management unit (MMU) to provide virtual memory services to software threads (such as Linux does), additional effort is required to enable hardware threads to directly share their virtual addresses with software threads, and to take advantage of the benefits of virtual memory, such as memory protection and on-demand paging.

Figure 4.6 shows three techniques to enable shared memory operations between hardware and software threads, each with various levels of transparency to the developer:

Direct access to physical memory from user space (Figure 4.6(a)): Through a special kernel module, the system can grant user space processes direct access to the physical memory space of the system. However, this approach has several drawbacks: user space programs may accidentally or maliciously overwrite other processes' or the kernel's data structures, effectively crashing the system or at least circumventing the memory protection mechanisms; shared data segments must be explicitly allocated to be used by hardware and software threads, or they must be located outside of the regular system's memory space; and memory performance is significantly reduced when accessing physical memory through a dedicated kernel module.

Kernel memory (DMA buffers) (Figure 4.6(b)): Similar to the first method, threads can use special kernel memory areas, so-called DMA buffers, for shared memory. These regions of memory are originally intended for direct memory transfers between peripheral components and their associated kernel drivers, and are mapped to a contiguous region within the memory space reserved by the kernel. Because the offset between a DMA buffer's logical and physical addresses is always constant, address translation for memory accesses performed by hardware threads is cheap and straightforward. The amount of memory available for DMA buffers is, however, limited, and their allocation and access from software again requires a dedicated kernel module.

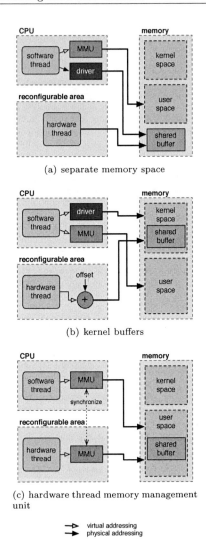

(a) separate memory space

(b) kernel buffers

(c) hardware thread memory management
unit

Figure 4.6: Three methods for sharing memory between hardware and software
threads. (a) A separate memory space is allocated for explicit access
by hardware and software. (b) Kernel buffers are used for data
sharing. (c) The hardware thread operates on virtual addresses
using a dedicated MMU.

Hardware support for virtual memory (Figure 4.6(c)): Instead of trying to access physical memory addresses from hardware, providing support for address translation from virtual to physical addresses within a dedicated hardware module promises the highest degree of transparency, albeit with the largest hardware overhead of the three described approaches. Such a hardware-thread memory management unit transparently maps virtual addresses to their physical equivalents as defined by the operating system's page tables, thus allowing hardware threads to share pointers and consequently data directly with software threads.

The third method has been successfully applied to reconfigurable hardware accelerators by Lange et. al. [67]. Adapting the approach to multithreaded hardware, we have implemented a hardware thread memory management unit (HWT-MMU) mirroring the MMU within the system's central PowerPC. The HWT-MMU comprises a translation look-aside buffer (TLB) to cache previous address translations, and is able to retrieve page table entries directly from the software kernel's page directory, located in main memory, in order to autonomously service page misses of the TLB without CPU interruption. Also, the HWT-MMU can be used to enforce memory access policies (e.g., memory protection); in this case, any unauthorized memory access from a hardware thread is directly forwarded to its delegate thread, which can handle the error condition using the host OS kernel's facilities. Section 5.1.2 provides details on our implementation of the HWT-MMU and its integration into the Linux kernel.

Hardware FIFOs

The bus access facilities provided by the OSIF permit the hardware thread to achieve high data transfer rates to and from main memory. While this mechanism represents an improvement over the indirect communication methods provided by the OS call relay technique (e.g., via mailboxes), its performance can suffer considerably when several threads, the CPU, or other peripherals are contending for the bus.

To allow for bus-independent thread-to-thread data communication, the ReconOS run-time environment provides dedicated FIFO buffers implemented in hardware. Two threads connected by such a FIFO module can transfer data without interrupting the CPU or increasing bus load. When a hardware thread signals a pending read or write access to such a FIFO, the OSIF's command decoder passes the request to the *FIFO manager* (see Figure 4.4), which controls the handshake lines of the FIFO modules. In the event of a write request to a full FIFO or a read request to an empty FIFO, the FIFO manager can also suspend the hardware thread's OS synchronization state machine, thus providing blocking *get/put* operations on FIFOs. Details on the performance of this message passing mechanism can be found in Section 7.2.4.

4.5 Software Integration

This section outlines the software mechanisms necessary to integrate the low-level communication and synchronization protocols provided by the OSIF into a multithreaded software environment. We present the mechanisms for thread creation and termination together with the necessary data structures for hardware thread management and resource sharing, and outline the tasks performed by the delegate threads.

4.5.1 Thread Creation and Termination

The creation of threads from within the ReconOS programming model is almost identical for software threads (`pthread_create()`) and hardware threads (`rthread_create()`). An example of the POSIX-like creation of both variants is shown in Listing 4.3. A hardware thread (or `rthread`, line 16) takes the same priority and stack size parameters as a software thread (or `pthread`, line 12). These parameters are encapsulated in a `pthread_attr` structure as declared on lines 13 and 17 for the software and hardware threads of the example, respectively. In hardware threads, `pthread_attr` is used for the associated delegate thread (see Section 4.5.3) and influences the hardware thread's priority when contending for access to operating system objects.

The main difference between the kernel data structures of software and hardware threads exists in details about the shared resources (lines 6ff.) and thread location. This additional information is stored in an `rthread_attr` structure, as declared on line 18, initialized on lines 25ff. and explained in Section 4.5.2. Creating a hardware thread using `rthread_create()` (line 39) consequently differs very little from creating a software thread using `pthread_create()` (line 31) as defined by POSIX—instead of an entry point into a software routine, a hardware thread is passed its `rthread_attr` structure.

In the static case considered throughout this chapter, creating a hardware thread using `rthread_create()` assumes that the hardware thread is already present in the reconfigurable fabric. Here, hardware threads are configured to the FPGA together with the static hardware architecture (e.g., buses and peripherals) during system bootup. To establish a direct mapping between a static hardware thread and its delegate, the `rthread_attr` structure contains a

```
1   // shared OS objects
2   mqd_t my_mqueue;
3   sem_t my_sem;
4
5   // resource array for hardware thread
6   reconos_res_t hwthread_resources[2] = {
7           { &my_mqueue, POSIX_MQD_T },
8           { &my_sem,    POSIX_SEM_T }
9   };
10
11  // software thread object and attributes
12  pthread_t       swthread;
13  pthread_attr_t swthread_attr;
14
15  // hardware thread object and attributes
16  rthread_t       hwthread;
17  pthread_attr_t hwthread_swattr;
18  rthread_attr_t hwthread_hwattr;
19
20  // initialization of software thread attributes
21  pthread_attr_init(&swthread_attr);
22
23  // initialization of hardware thread attributes
24  pthread_attr_init(&hwthread_swattr);
25  rthread_attr_init(&hwthread_hwattr);
26  rthread_attr_setresources(&hwthread_hwattr,
27                            hwthread_resources, 2);
28  rthread_attr_setslotnum(&hwthread_hwattr, 0);
29
30  // software thread creation
31  pthread_create(
32      &swthread,              // thread object
33      &swthread_attr,         // attributes
34      swthread_entry,         // entry point
35      ( void * ) data         // entry data
36  );
37
38  // hardware thread creation
39  rthread_create(
40      &hwthread,              // thread object
41      &hwthread_swattr,       // software attributes
42      &hwthread_hwattr,       // hardware attributes
43      ( void * ) data         // entry data
44  );
```

Listing 4.3: Creation of software and hardware threads using the POSIX and ReconOS APIs.

Name	Description
*resources	Array of OS resources used by thread
resources_count	Number of resources in *resources
fifoRead_resNum	Resource index mapping for read hardware FIFO
fifoWrite_resNum	Resource index mapping for write hardware FIFO
slot_num	Which slot this thread is running on
init_data	Initial data for thread initialization
init_fun()	Initialization function called on thread creation
exit_fun()	Cleanup function called on thread termination
flags	Internal thread flags

Table 4.4: Hardware thread attributes.

field referring to a specific slot number within the ReconOS system, which is set using `rthtread_attr_setslotnum()`, as done on line 28 of the example. With partial reconfiguration, as outlined in Chapter 6, the loading of a hardware thread's bitstream is implicitly done by the scheduler upon thread creation.

Table 4.4 lists all public and private hardware thread attributes stored within `struct rthread_attr`. Among pointers to the shared resources and the slot number associated with its hardware thread, it also stores initialization data and kernel flags, as well as mapping information for the OSIF's hardware FIFO connections (see Section 4.4.4). Furthermore, it is often necessary to allocate or initialize thread-specific data structures upon thread initialization. To simplify this mainly sequential process and avoid unnecessary complicated initialization states within a hardware thread's state machine, ReconOS hardware threads can be associated with *init* and *exit* functions, which are called on thread creation and termination, respectively, and are also referenced in the `rthread_attr` structure.

Thread termination can be initiated by the respective threads themselves using the functions `pthread_exit()` (within software threads) or `reconos_thread_-exit()` (within hardware threads). Alternatively, threads can be explicitly aborted from another thread using `pthread_kill()`. Apart from POSIX, hardware and software threads can also be created and terminated using the eCos API, if supported by the host operating system. Hardware threads use the same `rthread_attr` structure in both APIs.

4.5.2 Resource Sharing

In the multithreaded programming model, individual threads of an application perform their tasks in a parallel manner by sharing specific resources, such as data structures or synchronization primitives. In this context, a resource is any operating system object which can be interacted with from a thread, such as mutexes, message queues, or pointers.

Apart from memory, both the access to and the functionality of resources is controlled by the software operating system kernel; software threads invoke specific API functions to create and interact with a resource, such as `semaphore_post()` or `mq_recv()`. All these API calls take predefined data structures as arguments (e.g., `sem_t` or `mq_t`), which contain all necessary information for executing the desired behavior and applying the results to invoking threads, affected resources, and kernel-internal data. In purely software-based multithreaded applications, these data structures are typically allocated as global variables, which can be easily shared among threads.

A hardware thread, though enabled by the OSIF and its internal structure to call operating system functions, generally does not have the information necessary for direct interaction with operating system resources. As semaphores, mutexes, message queues, and even most shared memory buffers are explicitly created in software before starting the application's threads, they do not exist at the time of hardware thread synthesis. Even though it is in many cases possible to analyze the software executable of an application, extract the addresses of resource data structures from its symbol table, and include them in the hardware thread's VHDL description by means of a package or a separate preprocessing step, this approach is not feasible: in the case of a change in the layout of the executable, for example caused by the inclusion of additional global variables or functions, all hardware threads using the resource would need to be re-synthesized, which takes considerable time. Some resources might even be dynamically created at run-time, effectively ruling out any design-time mapping of resource information between hardware and software.

Consequently, a run-time mechanism is necessary for the sharing of operating system resources. To provide hardware thread designers with a mechanism of comparable simplicity to global variables, we have developed an explicit mapping process which relates numeric identifiers used by a hardware thread to so-called *resource arrays* maintained by the software operating system kernel. This resource array maintains a collection of all resources accessible by the respective hardware thread. All ReconOS hardware API functions feature a numeric call parameter identifying a specific resource, which is typically aliased by a symbolic VHDL constant for ease of use within the hardware thread's OS synchronization state machine. Figure 4.7 illustrates the relationship between this identifier and the thread's resource array. Upon receiving an OS call request from its hardware thread (1), a delegate can use the resource identifier as an index into the resource array (2) to retrieve the corresponding address or data structure (3) and use it to execute the appropriate operating system

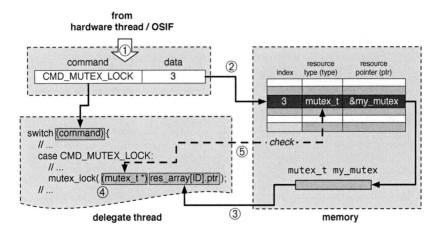

Figure 4.7: Resource array for referencing OS resources. Each hardware OS call refers to an entry in a resource table, which is used in the corresponding software OS call.

call (4). The definition of the resource array—and thus the mapping between symbolic VHDL constants and actual objects of the operating system kernel—is established at design time; an example can be seen in Listing 4.3 (line 6). This technique also transparently separates the hardware thread API from the API used to define the OS objects (e.g., the eCos kernel API or the POSIX API), and it provides a concise overview of the resources used by the individual threads.

As a consequence of this mechanism, a single hardware thread description (i.e., VHDL source code, netlist or possibly a relocatable bitstream) can be used for multiple instances in the system; giving different instances access to different resources is simply a matter of changing the delegate's resource array.

Because the resource array contains not only a pointer to the specific resource, but also a field identifying its distinct type, the delegate is able to perform run-time error checking (5). Access to incompatible resource types is reported to the operating system. As will be shown in Section 5.2.2, the actual error handling code is generated from ReconOS' command definitions, which avoids any accidental introduction of errors or omission of correct type checking when manually adding new hardware API calls.

4.5.3 Delegate Threads

A fundamental assumption of the ReconOS programming model concerns the transparency of thread-to-thread communication and synchronization, regardless of the execution context (hardware or software) of the respective communication partners. If A and B are communicating threads, A does not need to know whether B is a software thread executing on the CPU, or a hardware thread mapped to the FPGA, and vice versa. This enables the designer to easily replace, for instance, a software thread with a functionally equivalent hardware thread, thus achieving the desired flexibility of design space exploration with respect to the hardware/software partitioning.

In ReconOS, this transparency is achieved through the concept of *delegate threads*. The delegate is responsible for executing operating system calls on behalf of the corresponding hardware thread, making it appear as a software thread to the operating system kernel. It bridges the remaining gap between the OSIF's control bus registers and the operating system kernel and essentially represents the software counterpart for the OSIF, as it contains generic interface functionality commonly required by all hardware threads, regardless of their specific function. A delegate thread for a statically configured ReconOS system performs three fundamental tasks[1]:

- Initialization of the associated OSIF

- Retrieval, decoding, and execution of incoming OS call requests

- Transfer of an OS call's return value back to the OSIF

When creating a ReconOS hardware thread using `rthread_create()`, the ReconOS library code instantiates a regular software thread, whose entry point is the delegate thread code common to all hardware threads, and sets and initializes the additional kernel structures for hardware threads with parameters derived from the `rthread_attr` structure described in Section 4.5.1. It also registers the hardware interrupt for the associated slot, and sets up the internal OS-specific synchronization mechanism between OSIF and delegate thread, before finally releasing the delegate thread to be executed by the OS scheduler.

A delegate thread always operates in the same iterative manner, the exact nature of which is dependent on the host operating system kernel. The following gives a conceptual overview of a delegate's mode of operation, which is also depicted in Figure 4.8; Section 5.1 provides further, implementation-specific details of the process.

---

[1] In a dynamically configured ReconOS system, a delegate also interfaces with the reconfiguration logic and is responsible for saving and restoring thread state (see Section 6.5).

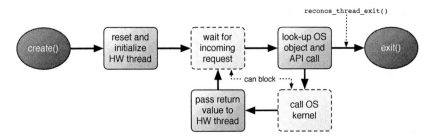

Figure 4.8: Execution flow of a delegate thread. A delegate is responsible for initializing the hardware thread and continuously relaying all incoming OS calls to the software kernel.

After invocation by the OS' software scheduler, it sends initialization commands to its associated OSIF, which involves resetting OSIF internal state and the hardware thread circuitry, as well as the transfer of initialization data (`init_data`) to the hardware thread. After initialization, the delegate thread enters a loop, where it continuously waits for an incoming OS call request, which is signaled by a slot- and OS-specific synchronization mechanism posted by the associated interrupt handler. The call parameters are then retrieved from the OSIF control bus registers, and the corresponding OS call is executed using the native API of the software kernel. Depending on the nature of the call, the hardware thread's OS synchronization state machine remains stalled during call execution, as previously explained in Section 4.3.2; this is for example true for any calls requiring a return value. Upon return of the OS routine, the OSIF is notified and any applicable return value is passed back to the hardware before the delegate waits again for the next incoming OS call.

Because commands and data are transferred to and from the OSIF registers using sequential non-atomic operations, accesses to the OSIF are uniformly protected by an OSIF-associated mutex. In a multithreaded environment, this is necessary to avoid data corruption caused by scheduling events during an OSIF transfer.

4.6 Chapter Conclusion

This chapter has outlined the concepts and mechanisms for designing and executing hardware threads. We have shown how the OS interaction of a hardware module written in VHDL can be structured within an intuitive state machine description without impeding the potential for fine-grained parallelism. A dedicated operating system interface (OSIF) module connects the hardware threads to the system's hardware architecture and provides low-level services for data communication and OS call relaying. We have also detailed the necessary mechanisms for resource sharing and hardware thread control available to software threads. Together, this infrastructure of methods and components allows hardware threads to be transparently integrated into a multithreaded environment.

The previous chapters covered both the concepts and general architecture of a multithreaded hardware/software system. The implementation and integration into existing software operating systems and associated tools for synthesis, simulation, and debugging are detailed in the next chapter.

CHAPTER 5

Implementation and Tool Flow

This chapter describes the implementation of the concepts presented in the previous chapters within existing operating systems, as well as details about the associated tool flow for synthesizing a multithreaded hardware/software system. We also present techniques and tools for simulating hardware threads, and monitoring and in-system debugging of a complete implemented ReconOS system. As in the previous chapter, the topics discussed here refer to statically assembled ReconOS systems. The extensions necessary for dynamic reconfiguration are deferred to Chapter 6.

Section 5.1 shows in detail how the communication mechanisms between OS kernel and OS interface are integrated into eCos and Linux, two host kernels of different designs. Section 5.2 introduces and explains our tool chain for assembling a complete system of hard- and software threads.

5.1 Host Operating Systems

Following the concepts presented in the previous chapters, we have integrated the necessary extensions for supporting hardware threads into two existing operating systems: eCos and Linux. While eCos is targeted primarily at the embedded segment, and consequently focuses on compactness and low resource utilization, Linux can be applied to a wider range of target platforms, but also requires considerably more resources, both in terms of memory and computational performance.

5.1.1 eCos

The eCos [40] real-time operating system provides a modular and configurable framework of operating system services. Application designers can select the necessary packages from the eCos repository and compile them into a library, which the final application is statically linked against. eCos is also configurable on a source code level. Through the extensive use of preprocessor macros, unneeded code is removed at compile time, resulting in small code sizes and memory footprints, which suit the targeted embedded segment. eCos components are written in a combination of C, C++ and assembler, while the eCos kernel itself is implemented in C++. eCos supports a range of target processor architectures, including the PowerPC 405, but not the MicroBlaze soft core. Currently, this limits applying eCos to Xilinx FPGAs of the Virtex-II Pro, Virtex-4 FX and Virtex-5 FXT families.

To transparently include ReconOS delegate threads in the eCos programming model, we have extended the eCos thread class `Cyg_Thread` to include additional information relevant to hardware threads, such as OSIF addresses, interrupt numbers, and OS object tables. Together with C wrappers for thread creation that are very similar to the eCos own `cyg_thread_create()` and POSIX' `pthread_create()` API, reusing the existing kernel code allows ReconOS delegate threads (and, by extension, the associated hardware threads) to take advantage of all services provided by the eCos kernel. To remain portable across different host operating systems, application designers are encouraged to primarily use functions from the POSIX compatibility package that comes with eCos.

Because eCos does not distinguish between user and kernel space but runs entirely in the processor's real mode, hardware access from user threads is greatly simplified. Although the delegate thread is logically part of the user application rather than the kernel, it can directly access the control bus to communicate with its corresponding OSIF. eCos also lets hardware and software threads share the same address space, since it disables the MMU, sacrificing memory protection and privilege management for a greatly simplified memory access model and higher performance. While unreasonable for larger-scale multiuser systems, this is entirely appropriate for small-footprint self-contained embedded systems, as targeted by eCos.

The sequence of events that is performed to relay an OS call from hardware to the eCos kernel is shown in Figure 5.1. When a hardware thread uses a VHDL API call to request an operating system service, the respective VHDL procedure asserts certain handshake lines between the thread and its OSIF (1). Pending OS calls requested by the OSIF are signaled to the CPU's interrupt

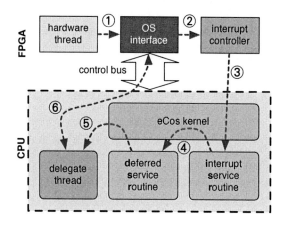

Figure 5.1: Communication between hardware threads and delegate threads in eCos. Interrupts are handled by ISR and DSR routines before waking up the delegate thread.

controller via a dedicated interrupt line (2). In eCos, interrupt processing is split into two steps to minimize interrupt latency. First, a minimal *interrupt service routine* (ISR) is invoked (3), which executes in its own context, performs the necessary operations to enable reception of the next interrupt as quickly as possible, and marks the *deferred service routine* (DSR) (4) for execution. The latter is scheduled by the regular eCos scheduler in order not to interfere with the low-level interrupt processing. As the last step before the actual delegate thread is invoked, the DSR posts a semaphore (5) which the delegate is waiting for, essentially signaling an incoming request. The delegate thread then directly accesses the OSIF's registers via dedicated control bus access instructions to retrieve call parameters (6) and executes the requested eCos kernel function. Section 7.2.2 evaluates the timing overhead of this OS call sequence.

All interrupt handlers, service routines, delegate thread code, API wrappers and low-level access routines have been added to eCos as a separate configuration package that can be disabled or enabled like any other eCos package using standard configuration tools (see Section 5.2.2).

5.1.2 Linux

The Linux operating system is employed on a larger set of target architectures and therefore enjoys a wider adoption than eCos. The list of architectures includes the PowerPC 405 and the Xilinx MicroBlaze soft core. Supporting a MicroBlaze increases the range of ReconOS targets to include FPGAs without an embedded CPU core. For our MicroBlaze prototype, we have opted for the omission of the memory management unit, which simplifies memory transfers between software and hardware threads.

While offering a wide set of configurable options, the Linux kernel does not allow reducing its memory footprint as much as the eCos kernel does. Absolute values on the size of the respective kernel images are difficult to obtain, as the code size greatly depends on the selected features, the target architecture, and the employed compiler. Also, an eCos kernel image already includes all necessary API implementations, the libc, and possibly a network stack, and thus can range from as little as 25 kBytes to a few 100 kBytes. It can be expected that a Linux kernel's size exceeds an equivalent eCos kernel by about an order of magnitude.

The vast majority of existing Linux variants distinguishes between *kernel* or *supervisor mode*—where most operating system services are executed and which enjoys certain privileges, such as direct hardware access—and *user mode*—where all application-level code is executed while precisely observing memory access protocols and instruction-level privileges. Invoking operating system calls therefore implies a switch from user mode to kernel mode and back, which causes non-negligible delays in OS object access times in Linux compared to those of eCos.

To communicate with its OSIF, a delegate thread needs access to the control bus. On a PowerPC system, this is accomplished through the `mtdcr` and `mfdcr` instructions, both of which are *privileged*. As mentioned earlier, user-space code, such as a delegate thread, typically cannot execute privileged instructions. To make the OSIF registers accessible to the delegate, we have implemented the low-level hardware access to the OSIF registers in a kernel driver, which publishes the registers through a device node, as depicted in Figure 5.2. The hardware-independent code, such as the API wrappers and the delegate thread code, is implemented through a library that is linked with the user application.

Due to the separation of hardware-dependent and independent code, the sequence of events to relay an OS call from hardware to the Linux kernel differs from the one described for the eCos kernel. The signal assertions between hardware thread and OSIF (1) and the interrupt request to the system's interrupt controller (2) are identical. When a delegate thread needs to access its OSIF, it does so through filesystem accesses to the kernel driver's device node. In eCos, synchronization between the delegate thread and the OSIF was achieved through a dedicated semaphore. In Linux, this synchronization is implemented

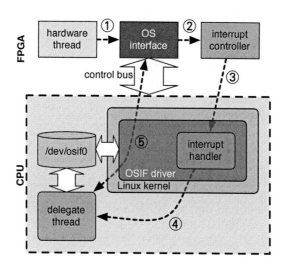

Figure 5.2: Communication between hardware threads and delegate threads in Linux. Since the delegate does not have direct hardware access, interrupt handling and OSIF access is handled by a kernel driver.

through read accesses blocking until an interrupt from the OSIF is registered (3). Only then the blocking delegate thread is resumed (4) and the read access translated into control bus operations (5). Essentially, the delegate thread is constantly blocking on a read from the OSIF device node, combining communication and synchronization in one operation. Write operations to an OSIF do not block. The timing overhead of this sequence is analyzed in Section 7.2.2.

A welcome side effect when using Linux is the richer environment in which user applications can execute. Apart from a wider range of software libraries and helper applications, debugging is already simplified through the availability of a shell with which to start separate applications instances and debugging/-monitoring tools. However, this does not come without a performance penalty in software operations due to more complex scheduling, necessarily running system daemons and an increased memory footprint.

Virtual Memory

As previously discussed, data transfers between software and hardware threads are complicated by the fact that most Linux implementations employ virtual

81

memory. This means that blocks of shared memory used to transfer data to or from hardware threads are not necessarily contiguous, and are addressed using virtual addresses, which need to be translated into physical addresses by memory management units (MMUs), both for software threads within the CPU as well as for hardware threads within the OSIF. Usually, this address translation process is not done for individual memory words, but for larger *pages* of a certain granularity or *page size.*

We have implemented a hardware thread MMU (HWT-MMU) for hardware threads that integrates closely with the Linux kernel and is able to handle the following tasks:

Address translation: Using a translation-look-aside buffer (TLB) to cache previous address translations, the HWT-MMU can quickly compute the physical page addresses for memory transactions requested by the hardware thread.

Page table walk: On a TLB miss, the HWT-MMU can autonomously walk through the Linux kernel's page tables to retrieve mappings between virtual and physical memory pages.

Access control: Upon unauthorized memory accesses initiated by the hardware thread, the HWT-MMU reports the error condition back to the delegate thread, where it is handled by the host operating system's memory subsystem.

Figure 5.3 shows how the HWT-MMU is integrated into the ReconOS hardware architecture. All memory accesses initiated by the hardware thread use virtual memory addresses, which are transparently translated by the HWT-MMU integrated into the OSIF. The HWT-MMU has direct access to the kernel's page tables stored in main memory and caches its hardware thread's address mappings in a separate TLB, which can also be accessed across the system's control bus. The TLB itself is implemented as a content-addressable memory (CAM) containing the virtual page numbers (tags) and a data memory containing the associated physical page numbers and access attributes. A memory-mapping already cached in the TLB can be asynchronously retrieved in less than a clock cycle.

The process of serving virtual memory accesses is illustrated in Figure 5.4. If the mapping between the requested virtual memory address and its physical address exists in the TLB (TLB hit), the corresponding access attributes are checked and, if the access is valid, the memory access is performed using the physical address. If the TLB does not contain the requested address mapping (TLB miss), the associated page table entry (PTE) is read from main memory

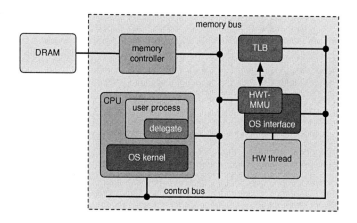

Figure 5.3: HWT-MMU architecture [13]. The HWT-MMU transparently handles the OSIF's memory communication and caches page mappings in the TLB. It also has access to the OS kernel's page tables stored in main memory.

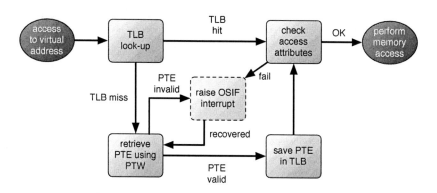

Figure 5.4: HWT-MMU operation [13]. Page mappings not stored in the TLB are retrieved directly from the kernel's page tables in memory. Error conditions are handled by the delegate in software.

through a page table walk (PTW) of the kernel's page table hierarchy. If a valid PTE is found, it is cached in the TLB and subsequently used. If no valid PTE can be found, or if a memory access is performed on a page with invalid access attributes, the request is forwarded to software by raising the OSIF interrupt. If it can be resolved within the kernel (e.g., by paging in the missing page from external storage), the memory access is continued with a page table walk within the HWT-MMU. The overheads incurred by the HWT-MMU are quantitatively evaluated in Section 7.2.4.

To ensure coherency between the page tables used by the HWT-MMU's page table walk—which are stored in main memory—and the page table entries used by the linux kernel—which may reside inside the CPU caches—, we have extended the Linux cache flush architecture so that it flushes the CPU's data cache and invalidates the HWT-MMU's TLB on every software-side modification of the kernel's page tables. To avoid unnecessary invalidations, the HWT-MMU's TLB also stores the process ID of the currently associated ReconOS/Linux process.

5.2 System Synthesis

This section presents details on the process and associated tools for assembly, synthesis and compilation of a ReconOS application. Starting with an overview of the tool chain, we show how descriptions of an application's hard- and software threads are assembled together with a top-level system specification to form a complete ReconOS system.

Using the multithreaded programming model, it is now possible to follow an intuitive, incremental design flow, as depicted in Figure 5.5:

- Initially, the application is developed completely in software, usually on a development workstation, which provides more convenient debugging facilities for establishing the application's functionality.

- Either during the initial design, or as a subsequent step, the software application is decomposed into separate threads, which communicate and synchronize using the programming model primitives described in Section 3.2. The application can be tested both on a development workstation and on the target platform.

- As the next step, the designer identifies the software threads with the most parallelization potential, possibly with the help of conventional profiling tools, and designs equivalent hardware thread implementations using the same programming model primitives, which are invoked using the

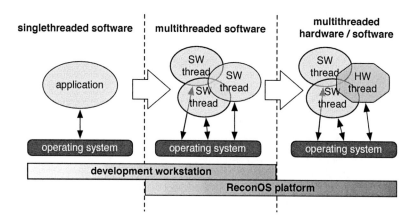

Figure 5.5: Incremental design flow. Applications can be prototyped on a development workstation and subsequently multithreaded and moved to the target platform, where individual software threads can be turned into hardware threads.

ReconOS API. During testing, the hardware and software threads can be seamlessly exchanged or duplicated, and the resulting HW/SW partitioning evaluated on the target platform. This allows for greatly simplified design space exploration.

The hardware generation process is mostly identical for both of our supported host operating systems, whereas the software portion of the tool chain is explained separately for each variant.

While the assembly of a ReconOS system requires custom tools, we rely on standard tool flows for the individual back-end synthesis and compilation of the hardware and software components of the system, respectively. Based on a regular Xilinx Embedded Development Kit (EDK) project structure, the final bitstream for FPGA configuration is generated using off-the-shelf synthesis and implementation tools. Similarly, the source code for an application's software threads as well as the operating system kernel and associated ReconOS libraries are compiled and linked using a regular GNU C compiler (GCC) tool chain. It is in the preceding stages of the system assembly process and in the custom packages and libraries which augment the host operating system that the specifics of the ReconOS build process become apparent.

Typically, the ReconOS tool flow first builds the hardware architecture — including the hardware threads—of a ReconOS system before compiling the software, since specific parts of the ReconOS support libraries depend on detailed knowledge of specific hardware parameters, such as OSIF base addresses and interrupt vectors.

5.2.1 Hardware

The general tool flow for generating the hardware components of a ReconOS system is shown in Figure 5.6. It starts from a reference design prepared for the individual target platform, which is in itself synthesizable and provides a test bed for software-only implementations of the application, as well as a starting point for the iterative design process promoted by ReconOS, in which software threads are subsequently profiled and translated into hardware. The reference design is given as a standard Xilinx EDK project, which custom tools modify according to the system specification provided as a PRJ file by the application designer (see Appendix A.4). The applied modifications include instantiations of OSIFs and hardware threads and connections to existing memory and control bus interfaces as well as to the system's interrupt controller. During this process, the tools are capable of adapting to unconventional system topologies (multiple data buses etc.). The whole process is source-transparent in the sense that the user can easily modify the system description by hand at intermediate steps of the generation process, for example to allow for custom external thread ports. The resulting completed ReconOS project is then processed by Xilinx' platgen tool, which generates a top-level VHDL description together with VHDL wrappers and a synthesis script for all sub-components of the system. Using standard FPGA synthesis and implementation tools, we then generate a static bit stream suitable for configuration of the target platform's FPGA.

The ReconOS repository provides a number of reference designs for our prototype target platforms. Depending on the requirements of the application, these reference designs contain various combinations of peripherals, such as network, display, and other I/O controllers, and consequently offer different amounts of free logic resources to be used for the implementation of hardware threads. From the hardware perspective, supporting a new target platform is simply a matter of adding a new reference design, which can usually be derived directly from manufacturer-provided example designs or board support packages (BSPs). To be suitable for the generation of a static ReconOS system, a reference design must at least include a CPU supported by the host operating system, a main memory bus, a control bus, and an interrupt controller.

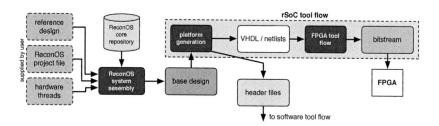

Figure 5.6: ReconOS hardware tool flow. The platform description needed by the regular rSoC tool flow is automatically generated from a ReconOS application description.

Different communication topologies are possible, but may need manual system assembly or a suitable porting of the system generation tools.

Hardware threads are described by one or more VHDL files, with the hardware thread's top level entity including the OSIF interface signals defined in Table 4.3 (p. 60). The thread description is then wrapped in a Xilinx EDK compatible IP core description, which is later incorporated in the system assembly process. The generation of the EDK wrapper is automatically handled by the tool chain, which supports hardware threads written purely in VHDL as well as thread descriptions containing both VHDL code and pre-synthesized netlists.

5.2.2 Software

Depending on the way a target software application and its host operating system is assembled, ReconOS provides its software API and functionality either through OS integrated packages or through kernel drivers and a user-space library. The following paragraphs describe the integration of the respective software components into our implemented host operating systems, eCos and Linux.

ReconOS/eCos

Due to the fact that eCos is targeted at the embedded software segment, applications deployed using eCos are represented by a single, monolithic executable, rather than a kernel, dynamic libraries, and run-time loadable process images. In other words, an eCos system typically runs a single process at a time, and

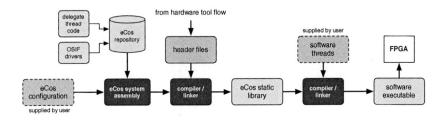

Figure 5.7: ReconOS/eCos software tool flow. The eCos software repository is extended with delegate routines and OSIF drivers and statically linked to the user's software source code.

generally does not allow dynamic loading of code that was not present at system compile-time. Consequently, the compilation of an eCos application involves first creating a static library containing all code relating to operating system services, which is then linked against the compiled object files of the actual application using these services.

The major differentiating feature of eCos is its configurability at the source code level. Using an elaborate system of hierarchic configuration files (specified in a language called CDL) and several custom tools, application developers can specify the feature set of the created eCos library at a fine granularity and without incurring run-time overheads.

eCos groups related functionalities, such as POSIX compatibility functions, mathematic libraries, networking protocol stacks, or hardware drivers in logic groups called packages. In order to provide ReconOS' functionality to eCos developers in a transparent way, we have integrated its functionality—consisting of thread creation API, data structures, initialization functions, delegate thread code, and hardware interface routines—in its own eCos package. It can be configured in the same fine-granular way as other eCos packages to exclude selected ReconOS functionality not required by an individual application.

During compilation, a parsing tool integrated via CDL files into the eCos build process generates the delegate thread code from the command definition files explained in Section 5.2.2. Also, hardware paramaters such as OSIF memory addresses and interrupt vectors are extracted from the modified hardware design generated in the hardware implementation step (see Section 5.2.1). After compiling and linking both the eCos library and the application code, the resulting executable is typically loaded using the FPGA's JTAG debugging interface, although other mechanisms, such as boot loaders, are also feasible. Figure 5.7 depicts the complete software tool flow for a ReconOS/eCos system.

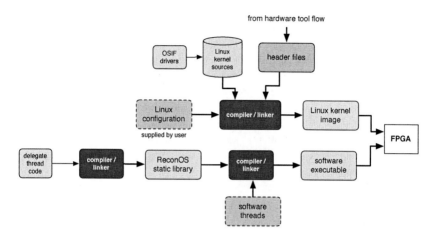

Figure 5.8: ReconOS/Linux software tool flow. The OSIF driver code is integrated into the kernel. The delegate thread code runs in user space and is linked as a library to the user application.

ReconOS/Linux

In contrast to eCos, a Linux system provides a vastly more flexible, and consequently more complex, execution environment for software. Instead of statically linking application code and OS functionality during compile-time, most Linux applications are contained in independent executable process images, which interact with operating system services through special system calls provided by dynamic libraries and the Linux kernel run-time environment. To execute a Linux application on an embedded system such as our prototype FPGA boards, we therefore need to load and boot the kernel first before logging into the system and executing the application. Thus, the compilation of the kernel and of the ReconOS application are two independent steps, depicted in Figure 5.8.

The ReconOS-specific functionality is split between a kernel module and a user-space library. The kernel module, which provides delegate threads with a means to access OSIF hardware registers, as described in Section 5.1.2, can either be compiled statically into the kernel, or loaded dynamically after booting the system. Unlike the eCos OSIF interface code, the kernel module retrieves hardware parameters, such as memory addresses and interrupt vectors, at boot or load time from the Linux device tree. This allows changing the hardware memory layout without recompiling the Linux kernel, significantly shortening the software development cycle. The ReconOS user-space library contains the delegate thread's code, which interacts with the hardware through the kernel module, as well as the thread management API and related data structures. Because the library provides generic interfaces both toward the software (via the predefined API) and the hardware (via the kernel module), it does not need to be recompiled when changing the hardware design or the software application.

The actual ReconOS software application code uses the defined API provided by the user-space library, which is identical to the API provided by the eCos package from the previous section, and thus is exactly the same for both Linux and eCos targets.

Delegate Thread Code Generation

One advantage of the concept of using delegate threads for relaying OS calls from hardware to the OS kernel is its flexibility. Supporting a new operating system call for hardware threads only requires an additional hardware API function in the ReconOS VHDL package, the definition of the associated command encoding in the OSIF protocol, and the implementation of the associated software API call inside the delegate thread's code.

To simplify and consolidate all operating system calls in a single place, we have integrated a code generator in the ReconOS software tool chain. Upon compilation of the ReconOS software packages and support libraries, the ReconOS tools regenerate the delegate thread code from a set of command definition files. The command definitions specify the name and encoding of a ReconOS operating system call, along with associated flags (e.g., whether the call can block or returns a value upon completion). Also included in the command definition are software code templates for calling the appropriate system call of the software kernel. These templates encapsulate the command-specific code fragments of the delegate thread for different target resource types, for which the individual software calls may differ across different API sets or host operating systems. For instance, the mail box primitive (`reconos_mbox_put()`), which provides a convenient way for passing pointers between threads, has a direct mapping to eCos mailboxes, but must be emulated using message queues when using POSIX message queues, e.g., within Linux, which does not support the eCos kernel API. The syntax of a command definition file is detailed in Appendix A.1.

The generation of the delegate thread code is performed by the Cheetah [92] template preprocessor, which extracts the necessary information from the command definition files and assembles the complete delegate thread code for the respective target operating system.

5.3 Hardware Thread Simulation

The ReconOS programming model suggests an incremental tool flow, in which an application is first realized completely in software, and then gradually divided into threads, of which the ones most amenable to parallelization in hardware are turned into ReconOS hardware threads. While software threads can be developed and debugged using standard tools, the inclusion of hardware threads leaves only two alternatives for functional validation of the complete application: simulation using a hardware simulator like ModelSim, or in-system debugging on the target platform. In this section, we focus on the former, while an approach for the latter is discussed in the succeeding section.

The non-negligible complexity of a ReconOS system, complete with peripherals, OS interfaces, hardware threads, processors, and associated software makes the simulation of the entire system quite unwieldy; the simulation of the operating system startup sequence alone consumes significant time on the order of several hours. To simplify the validation of hardware threads without requiring a complete virtual platform of the final system, ReconOS provides a mechanism for simulating single hardware threads based on a bus functional model (BFM).

The original objective of a BFM [115], which is available for the PLB and OPB buses as employed by the Xilinx tools, is to verify that custom IP cores connected to these buses comply with the respective bus specifications. For this purpose, a bus protocol monitor continuously listens on the simulated bus and checks all occurring transactions for timing, alignment, control signaling, and other errors. To speed up the simulation, a bus functional model replaces elaborate simulation models for memory controllers and microprocessors with simulated memory areas and a mechanism to initiate standard-compliant bus transactions from a simulated master. This master is driven by a bus functional language (BFL), which specifies the sequence of transactions. Figure 5.9(a) shows the layout of a typical BFM simulation system.

The ReconOS tool chain extends this existing bus functional model to assist application designers during hardware thread development and thus provides a robust simulation environment for hardware threads, as shown in Figure 5.9(b). We connect a single OSIF and the hardware thread under test to a BFM of the memory and control buses to form a simulation model of greatly reduced complexity when compared to the entire system. Instead of simulating the software operating system, the thread designer specifies the interactions between oper-

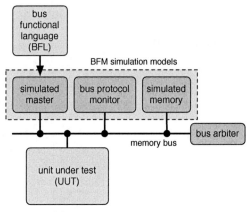

(a) regular bus functional model

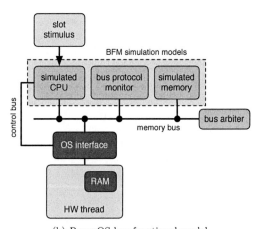

(b) ReconOS bus functional model

Figure 5.9: BFM simulation layout. The regular bus functional model (a) is modified to provide a simulated CPU capable of mimicking the delegate thread's bus activity (b).

ating system and hardware threads using a simple scripting language called *slot stimulus* (SST). In such a slot stimulus file, we list the OS interactions expected of the hardware threads together with their timing parameters. The simulated master, which now resembles a simulated CPU, generates the corresponding bus transactions and validates the responses from the simulated OSIF and hardware thread against the slot stimulus. While providing complete observability of the internal signals of a hardware thread, this mechanism also allows for creating automated test benches for regression testing the operating system interface during development of ReconOS itself.

```
 1  # wait for reset and initialization
 2  wait 1300 ns
 3
 4  write_unlock
 5  wait 100 ns
 6
 7  # mq_receive(MQUEUE_IN1, offset=0, size=16)
 8  read_mq_receive 00000000 00000000 16
 9  wait 500 ns
10  write_unlock 10000000
11
12  # wait for execution
13  wait 1 us
14
15  # sem_wait(SEM_READY)
16  read_sem_wait 00000001
17  wait 500 ns
18  write_unlock 10000000
19  wait 1500 ns
20
21  # sem_post(SEM_NEW)
22  read_sem_post 00000002
```

Listing 5.1: Example slot stimulus file.

Listing 5.1 shows an example slot stimulus file for the hardware thread introduced in Section 4.3.2 (Listing 4.2, p. 56)). The corresponding simulation output—including activity on the control and memory buses as well as important OSIF and thread signals—is shown in Figure 5.10. At the top of the figure, the control bus activity is annotated with the corresponding SST commands. Also, the relationship between the thread's FSM states and the thread's requests is indicated on the lower end of the figure. Note that because of the nature of the FSM description during blocking or busy states, the **state** signal indicates the *next active* state of the thread, and thus may not always corre-

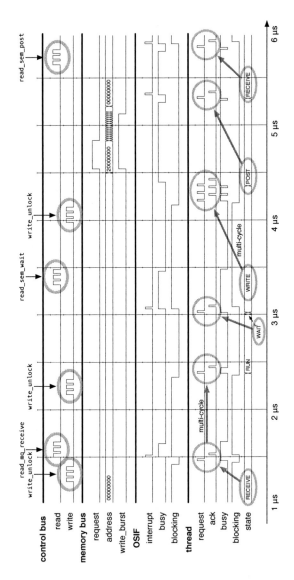

Figure 5.10: BFM simulation trace for the example of Listing 5.1.

spond directly to the currently executed OS call. The sequence of simulation events is as follows:

- The first event of the simulation is an `unblock` command (simulation time 1.3 μs, line 4 of Lisiting 5.1), which causes the *blocking* signal from the OSIF to go low.

- This allows the hardware thread to start and initiate a blocking, multi-cycle `mqueue_receive()` OS call. This call is then read from the control bus (1.5 μs, line 8) and simulated to return after 0.5 μs with another `unblock` command (2.1 μs, line 10).

- The hardware thread then computes its results in the RUN state and subsequently calls a `sem_wait()` OS function (3 μs), which is retrieved by the simulation model (3.3 μs, line 16) and returns with an `unblock` (4 μs, line 18).

- At 4.2μs simulation time, the hardware thread issues a burst write to system memory, which is handled in hardware and relayed to the memory bus. It does not correspond to any commands in the SST file. The hardware thread's FSM is suspended by the OSIF's *busy* signal during the memory transfer, which completes at 5.5 μs simulation time.

- Now, the hardware thread executes a `sem_post()` OS call, which is read by the simulation model (5.6 μs, line 22), and returns to the RECEIVE state.

The slot stimulus language contains equivalents of all ReconOS hardware API calls, as well as several simulation commands for OSIF initialization and control, as listed in Appendix A.2.

5.4 Monitoring and Debugging

While the simulation of a hardware thread using the aforementioned bus functional model allows the designer to verify the thread's functionality while observing its internal state, the behavior of the complete system cannot be examined this way. On the other hand, it is difficult to debug a hardware thread while running the complete application on the target platform, as hardware threads do not provide easily accessible debugging services known from the software development process and ranging from simple "printf()-debugging" to complex profiling and verification tools.

By augmenting the standard ReconOS system architecture with a run-time monitoring framework called *ReconoScope* [82], we provide an infrastructure

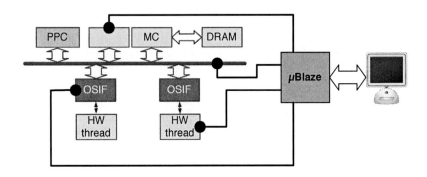

Figure 5.11: ReconoScope architecture. A separate processor connects to custom monitoring nodes to observe critical system components.

which enables us to accurately observe interactions between hardware threads, OSIF, and other system components such as the memory bus, thus providing assistance in debugging a complete system. As opposed to generic logic analyzers like Xilinx' ChipScope, our approach incorporates information about low-level OS services and protocols, and it can be integrated with the actual system under observation. Such a system can be used to provide run-time performance data to the main operating system kernel in order to identify bottlenecks and potentially adapt the hardware architecture to compensate for run-time data dependencies.

The run-time monitoring framework entails a separate SoC-like architecture shown in Figure 5.11. Specialized monitoring nodes gather relevant information, such as bus utilization, thread/OSIF interactions, or generic signal and event timing information. Using a separate bus, the information is relayed to a MicroBlaze CPU core, which collects and accumulates the monitoring node's data and maintains statistical information such as frequency, duty cycle, or average values that can be retrieved by an external interface.

ReconoScope provides simple and well-defined interfaces to its infrastructure and can be extended with user-defined monitoring nodes to enable custom data-gathering and in-system analysis. Figure 5.12 shows the composition of typical monitoring nodes together with their shared bus (DebugBUS) and MicroBlaze connections. The native frequency of the observed hardware modules often exceeds the processing capabilities of the monitoring system's MicroBlaze processor. To reduce the required data bandwidth and allow sequential processing of all monitoring node's data on the MicroBlaze, the incoming measurement

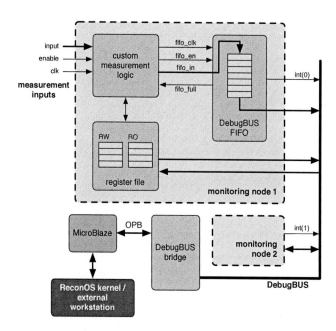

Figure 5.12: Composition of ReconoScope monitoring nodes [82]. Measurement data is preprocessed and buffered inside the monitoring node and can be retrieved by the CPU across the DebugBUS.

data is preprocessed in custom logic within the monitoring node, and buffered in a FIFO for later retrieval across the DebugBUS. Possible data preprocessing can entail, for example, averaging input data or deriving other statistical features from the incoming measurements. The data-reduction process can be configured from within the monitoring system by accessing a measurement node's internal registers across the DebugBUS.

The entire ReconoScope framework including CPU and monitoring buses and modules is encapsulated in custom IP cores and can be integrated into an existing ReconOS system using the Xilinx EDK. On such an augmented ReconOS system, the user can connect to the debugging system through a separate terminal interface and interactively monitor the system's activity. Figure 5.13 shows an example debugging session of the OSIF/hardware thread interface using ReconoScope, involving a OSIF protocol monitoring node (os2t 1/t2os 2) and a generic event trace core (Trac 3) for thread-specific signals. The out-

```
os2t 1:  05s 085,619,450ns UNBLOCK        step 0  Data: 0xAFFE1010
Trac 3:  05s 085,619,455ns 1b      1h     0b      0b    0b
t2os 2:  05s 085,619,455ns MBOX_GET                Data: 0x00000000           REQ
os2t 1:  05s 085,619,460ns UNBLOCK        step 0  Data: 0xAFFE1010           BUSY
Trac 3:  05s 085,619,465ns 0b      1h     0b      0b    0b
t2os 2:  05s 085,619,465ns MBOX_GET                Data: 0x00000000
os2t 1:  05s 085,619,470ns UNBLOCK        step 2  Data: 0x00000000           BUSY   BLOCK
os2t 1:  05s 085,637,210ns UNBLOCK        step 2  Data: 0x00000000           BLOCK
os2t 1:  05s 085,644,050ns UNBLOCK        step 2  Data: 0x001F5200           BLOCK  VALID
os2t 1:  05s 085,644,540ns UNBLOCK        step 2  Data: 0x001F5200           VALID
Trac 3:  05s 085,644,545ns 1b      1h     1b      1b    0b
t2os 2:  05s 085,644,545ns MBOX_GET                Data: 0x00000000           REQ
os2t 1:  05s 085,644,550ns UNBLOCK        step 2  Data: 0x001F5200           BUSY   VALID
Trac 3:  05s 085,644,555ns 1b      1h     1b      1b    0b
t2os 2:  05s 085,644,555ns MBOX_GET                Data: 0x00000000
os2t 1:  05s 085,644,560ns UNBLOCK        step 0  Data: 0xAFFE1010
Trac 3:  05s 085,644,565ns 1b      2h     0b      1b    0b
t2os 2:  05s 085,644,565ns READ_BURST              Data: 0x00000000           REQ
os2t 1:  05s 085,644,570ns UNBLOCK        step 0  Data: 0xAFFE1010           BUSY
Trac 3:  05s 085,644,575ns 0b      2h     0b      1b    0b
t2os 2:  05s 085,644,575ns READ_BURST              Data: 0x00000000
os2t 1:  05s 085,644,580ns UNBLOCK        step 1  Data: 0xAFFE1010
Trac 3:  05s 085,644,585ns 1b      2h     0b      1b    0b
t2os 2:  05s 085,644,585ns READ_BURST              Data: 0x001F5200           REQ
os2t 1:  05s 085,644,590ns UNBLOCK        step 1  Data: 0xAFFE1010           BUSY
Trac 3:  05s 085,644,595ns 0b      2h     0b      1b    0b
t2os 2:  05s 085,644,595ns READ_BURST              Data: 0x001F5200
os2t 1:  05s 085,644,600ns UNBLOCK        step 2  Data: 0xAFFE1010
Trac 3:  05s 085,644,605ns 1b      2h     1b      1b    0b
t2os 2:  05s 085,644,605ns READ_BURST              Data: 0x001F5210           REQ
os2t 1:  05s 085,644,610ns UNBLOCK        step 2  Data: 0xAFFE1010           BUSY
Trac 3:  05s 085,644,615ns 0b      2h     1b      1b    0b
t2os 2:  05s 085,644,615ns READ_BURST              Data: 0x001F5210
os2t 1:  05s 085,644,620ns UNBLOCK        step 0  Data: 0xAFFE1010           BUSY
os2t 1:  05s 085,645,480ns UNBLOCK        step 0  Data: 0xAFFE1010
Trac 3:  05s 085,645,485ns 1b      2h     0b      1b    0b
```

Figure 5.13: Example ReconoScope session [82]. Each monitored event is re-ported on a separate line, including the node's identifier (e.g., `Trac` 3), a timestamp, and a custom string representation of the event.

put from these three cores is distinguishable by the first column of the trace. In contrast to a logic analyzer like ChipScope, the employed monitoring nodes are able to decode the interface signals to provide more comprehensive debugging information such as transferred commands (e.g., `MBOX_GET`, `READ_BURST`, or `UNBLOCK`) and state flags (e.g., `REQ`, `BUSY`, or `BLOCKING`), and tag events with a system-wide time stamp.

5.5 Chapter Conclusion

In this chapter we have given a detailed overview of the integration of multithreaded hardware into the established software operating system kernels eCos and Linux. While eCos is targeted at embedded systems with tightly constrained resources—which shows in its configurability—, Linux provides a wider range of support for existing software components and hardware peripherals. We have explained in detail how our execution environment handles the specifics of the individual operating system (such as virtual memory management) while maintaining portability across different OS and CPU architectures. We have also shown how the generation process of a complete statically configured multithreaded CPU/FPGA system is managed from application description to bitstream upload by our end-to-end tool flow.

While previous chapters have focused on statically assembled ReconOS systems, the following chapter will introduce hardware multitasking concepts for reconfigurable hardware to enable the time-sharing of an FPGA's resources between hardware threads through partial reconfiguration.

CHAPTER 6

Hardware Multitasking

In this chapter, we motivate and present the hardware multitasking techniques and their implementations as employed by ReconOS.

Multithreaded programming is an increasingly popular way to express concurrency in applications. It allows to decompose an application into separate threads of execution, which can be synchronized using a defined set of programming model objects provided by an operating system. With the concurrency made explicit through the usage of threads, such an application can be mapped to a parallel execution environment, for example a multiprocessor machine. Often, when executing one or possibly many multithreaded applications at once, the number of threads may exceed the number of processing elements. In this case, a way has to be found to efficiently share the computing resources.

In fact, the original driving motivation behind the first applications of of multithreading was not the availability of multiple processing elements, but the ineffective utilization of a single processing unit when executing blocking operations, such as I/O. This lead to the development of various multitasking techniques to time-share the processing element between threads. Some of these techniques, although beneficial for single and even multi-processor systems executing software, are not as easily applicable in a heterogeneous environment of software threads executing on CPUs and hardware threads mapped to reconfigurable logic. Here, the reconfiguration architecture of the targeted platform FPGAs imposes restrictions on the time-sharing of hardware modules, requiring novel approaches of integrating hardware multitasking into the run-time system.

Section 6.1 motivates and differentiates the notions of multitasking and multi-threading as used in this thesis from common definitions found in the literature. In Section 6.2, we introduce the three most prominent techniques to execute multiple threads on a single processing element, and evaluate and discuss their applicability to the ReconOS environment in Section 6.3. Section 6.4 explains the necessary extensions to ReconOS hardware threads to enable their seamless reconfiguration, and Section 6.5 describes mechanisms for integrating hardware multitasking techniques into the host operating system. Finally, the augmented tool chain for the generation of a complete partially reconfigurable ReconOS system is outlined in Section 6.6.

6.1 Definitions

On the surface, the terms *multitasking* and *multithreading* both generally mean "executing multiple tasks at the same time". However, when looking at specialized areas such as processor architecture, parallel architectures, or operating systems, the two terms exhibit subtle differences. To avoid confusion, we shortly review typical occurrences of both expressions within the literature and clearly specify our definitions of them as used throughout this thesis.

The term *multithreading* finds regular but diverging uses within texts on computer architecture. For example, Hennessy and Patterson [51] define multi-threading as a mechanism that "allows multiple threads to share the functional units of a single processors in an overlapping fashion". Tanenbaum [103] describes how "on-chip multithreading allows the CPU to manage multiple threads of control at the same time". Both definitions are specific to single processor architectures. In the context of multiprocessor architectures, the concept of multithreading covers a broader area. Flynn [44], for example, defines multithreading to be the same as *shared resource multiprocessing* (SRMP), where multiple threads simultaneously executing on different processors may share certain resources, such as memory or special functional units. SRMP, however, does not necessarily involve the time-multiplexing of threads on a single processor.

The term *multitasking*, on the other hand, is commonly used in the context of operating systems, where multiple processes (or threads) have to be coordinated to achieve a *perceived* simultaneous execution on a *single* processing resource. Stallings [101], for example, describes multitasking as the technique of increasing system utilization by switching the processor between different programs or processes.

A common feature of the above uses of the term *multithreading* is the necessity to decompose an application into multiple concurrently executing threads, which can then be time-multiplexed on a single processor or be distributed among multiple processors. Consequently, in the following we will continue to use the term *multithreading* in a generalized way as a method to model applications with separate but interacting threads of execution—which could be applied to multithreaded single-processor architectures in the sense of Hennessy and Patterson, but also to parallel architectures as described by Flynn—and use *multitasking* when describing the specific mechanisms governing the time-sharing of single computational resources between multiple threads.

6.2 Multitasking Techniques

Conventional software operating systems employ several multitasking techniques with individual advantages and disadvantages and consequently varying areas of application. *Non-preemptive* techniques are comparatively easy to implement and simplify thread synchronization on uniprocessor systems, albeit at the cost of unpredictable latencies and no support for asynchronous operations. At the other end of the spectrum, *preemptive* multitasking enables the perceived simultaneous execution of multiple tasks on a single processor with low latencies, some level of predictability, and support for asynchronous (i.e., blocking) functions; it does, however, require elaborate synchronization schemes and incurs a substantial scheduling overhead.

The *non-preemptive* family of multitasking techniques includes *event-based programming*, a method that is popular within reactive systems (e.g., toolkits for graphical user interfaces), where a program needs to deal with multiple independent tasks responding to (possibly external) events. A central routine—sometimes called the *event loop*—dispatches incoming events to be handled by sequential subroutines. These subroutines then run to their completion, however long that may be. Most importantly, they cannot be interrupted or preempted, and will cause other event handling routines to wait. When reaching the end of such a subroutine, the control flow returns to the event loop, which then waits for another event to dispatch to a subroutine. This simple technique has several advantages: it is straightforward to implement; there are no thread preemptions which would require state information to be saved; synchronization between routines is implicit—there is no need for mutual exclusion; it provides excellent portability, since no multithreading support is required; and the scheduling overhead is minimal. However, non-preemptive multitasking also has significant drawbacks: most importantly, a long-running task will prevent other tasks from execution, which results in possibly long reaction times; subroutines cannot efficiently use blocking operating system routines, such as I/O—instead, they need to schedule a request with the central event loop and provide a callback function, often breaking the logical structure of the program; giving any guarantees regarding latencies or execution times is difficult and only possible under stringent assumptions about the nature of the subroutines.

In contrast, *preemptive multitasking* alleviates many of the disadvantages of non-preemptive multitasking. Here, different threads of execution can be preempted at arbitrary points in time. This approach allows to serve arriving high-priority threads with significantly lower latency, and is a prerequisite for many real-time scheduling algorithms such as earliest-deadline-first (EDF) or rate-monotonic (RM) scheduling [70]. However, the preemption of a thread requires the capability to determine and store a thread's state at any time during its execution, which is easy to achieve for software executing on a microprocessor, but difficult for custom hardware modules.

For a certain set of applications, there exists a middle ground in *cooperative* multitasking. This technique enables individual threads to voluntarily relinquish control of the processor to allow other threads to execute. With appropriately 'behaved' tasks, it can reduce latencies compared to non-preemptive methods, while, on uniprocessor systems, avoiding many of the synchronization pitfalls of preemptive multitasking. In software-based systems, though preemptive multitasking seems to be the more popular method for implementing multithreaded applications, cooperative techniques are still present within established programming languages, such as in Modula-II, Oberon, Simula, Lua, Python's *generator* functions, or Perl's *yield* statement. In fact, Moura et. al. [80] advocate the increased use of coroutines, which in essence are cooperatively executing functions, as a general control abstraction in modern programming languages.

6.3 Hardware Multitasking Concepts

The unique properties of a hardware thread implemented in an FPGA make it difficult to apply traditional multitasking schemes to enable resource-sharing between different threads of computation. A general-purpose microprocessor has a fixed set of registers, the contents of which define the physical state of the computational entity currently executing[1]. This makes it simple to suspend a computation and save its state; it is sufficient to transfer the register contents of

---

[1]Note that apart from the general purpose registers of a CPU, there may be additional information to be saved, such as, for instance, the state of the memory management unit.

the processor to memory. There is no need to store any information about the actual processing units, as they are identical for all computations performed on the device and cannot be modified. Also, the code saving the state is usually executed on the same processor as the suspended computation, and thus has direct access to the state information.

In contrast, a computation mapped onto an FPGA typically does not have an easily identifiable location defining its state. Instead, the state may be distributed across different storage elements (e.g., flip-flops, shift registers, or embedded memories) throughout the FPGA's fabric. In addition, not all storage elements may be used by a given configuration; indeed, not even all used storage elements may contribute to a computation's state. To make matters worse, there is no easy way to store the contents of a given computation's storage elements into memory, since the logic connected to the storage elements is dedicated to the computation itself. Thus, asynchronously saving and restoring state information, while possible, becomes increasingly difficult and requires the use of invasive or complex techniques such as scan chains or bitstream read-back. For example, Kalte et. al. [59] implement a mechanism using bitstream read-back to extract and later re-inject the contents of storage elements known to contain a task's state information. While flexible and transparent, this technique is dependent on extensive knowledge of the specific target device's bitstream format and may involve considerable overhead, since the contents of CLB registers can make up less than 1% of an FPGA's configuration bitstream. An alternative approach is the inclusion of register scan chains in a task's logic, as proposed by Jovanovic et. al. [58]. It does, however, incur a significant area and time overhead when preempting a task, as well as substantially reducing the tasks maximum operational frequency[2].

In the context of multithreaded systems for reconfigurable hardware, selecting an appropriate multitasking technique therefore becomes a more complex challenge.

6.3.1 Non-Preemptive Multitasking

The simple solution is not to interrupt threads during their execution at all, but letting them run from creation to termination. This is analogous to non-preemptive multitasking in uniprocessor software systems. ReconOS supports non-preemptive multitasking for hardware threads by providing `create()` and `exit()` calls within its API. When a hardware thread is created, its delegate thread requests the configuration of the appropriate bitstream to a free slot, if

---

[2]On a typical application (AES-128), Jovanovic showed a $\sim$30% area increase and a maximum frequency decrease of $\sim$20%.

available. In the same way, upon termination of a hardware thread, its delegate thread marks the slot as free, which allows another thread waiting for a slot to use it.

Let us consider a simple example of two hardware threads A and B, as depicted in Figure 6.1(a), with respective execution times of $T(A) = t_{A_0} + t_{A_1}$ and $T(B) = t_B$, and a reconfiguration time of t_l for either thread. Further, we can imagine that, during its execution, A calls a function which blocks for t_{block} until it returns. When run on a single slot using non-preemptive multitasking (Figure 6.1(b)), the total run time is:

$$T_n(A, B) = 2t_l + T(A) + t_{block} + T(B)$$

Thus, during the period t_{block}, thread A does not actively use the reconfigurable resources of its slot, which are nevertheless still blocked by it and unavailable for other threads.

6.3.2 Cooperative Multitasking

Seen in the light of the potential inefficiency of non-preemptive multitasking and the complexity of preempting reconfigurable hardware, cooperative multitasking techniques, while appearing unnecessarily handicapped in software-based systems given the easy availability of preemptive multitasking, present an acceptable compromise between processing efficiency and implementation complexity when applied to reconfigurable devices. Most of the difficulties in preempting hardware threads stem from the fact that in preemptive systems, a thread can be interrupted at arbitrary points during its execution. If we leave the actual decision to suspend a thread to the thread itself, it can select

- **what** state information to store, since the location and amount of that information is thread-specific,

- decide **how** to store the state by providing access logic only for the relevant state information, and

- choose **when** to suspend itself, sensibly picking a point in time when state information is minimal.

The last point is especially valuable for threads which frequently wait for data packages to process; during the (typically blocking) wait periods, such a thread often has minimal state information to be saved.

The logic requirements for the hardware thread in cooperative multitasking environments, while easier to implement than mechanisms for preemptive multitasking, are still higher than those for simple non-preemptive multitasking. At

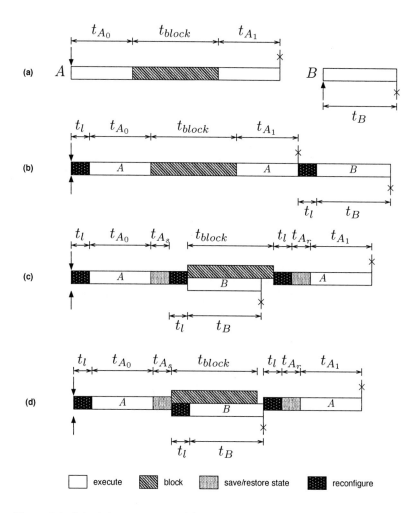

Figure 6.1: Scheduling example. (a) Threads with and without blocking call, (b) Non-preemptive multitasking, (c) Cooperative multitasking with reconfiguration *before* blocking, (d) Cooperative multitasking with reconfiguration *after* blocking.

the same time, cooperative multitasking offers better utilization of the reconfigurable resources than non-preemptive techniques, provided that the threads actually relinquish control (i.e., *yield*) of their computational resources.

A thread typically signals its readiness to be suspended by calling a `yield()` function. If no other threads are waiting for a slot, this call would return immediately with no consequences for the thread. Ideally, this is done just before periods in which the thread would not perform any computation anyway. An excellent point for relinquishing control are therefore blocking operating system calls.

In its simplest form, after suitable "yielding points" have been identified during design time, a thread could always store its state before reaching these points and then call a `yield()` function, regardless of whether there actually are any threads waiting for execution. This would essentially increase the thread's computation time by the state save/restore overhead for every `yield()` performed. A better approach is to check for other threads waiting for a slot before saving the state, thus only saving and restoring state, where necessary. Naturally, this only provides a benefit if the checking for other threads is less expensive than saving the state.

Let us revisit our previous example of threads A and B, shown in Figure 6.1(c). Now, instead of simply waiting for the blocking function call to return after t_{block}, A *yields* the slot to other waiting threads (in this case, B) after saving its state. This allows the operating system to remove A, reconfigure the waiting B into the (now free) slot, and start it before calling the blocking OS function for A. After B terminates and marks the slot as free, A is reconfigured, its state restored, and its execution resumed. The total run-time of both threads then amounts to:

$$T_c(A, B) = 3t_l + T(A) + t_{A_s} + t_{A_r} + max(t_{block}, T(B))$$

t_{A_s} and t_{A_r} are the times taken to save and restore A's state, respectively. The cooperative multitasking approach reduces the total run-time, provided that the reconfiguration overhead $t_l + t_{A_s} + t_{A_r}$ is less than both $T(B)$ and t_{block}:

$$T_c(A, B) < T_n(A, B) \Leftrightarrow \left\{ \begin{array}{l} t_l + t_{A_s} + t_{A_r} < T(B) \\ \wedge \quad t_l + t_{A_s} + t_{A_r} < t_{block} \end{array} \right.$$

Using this approach, reconfiguration of thread B takes place *before* calling the blocking OS function on behalf of A. Another conceivable strategy would first call the blocking function and then reconfigure the slot, as shown in Figure 6.1(d). This would lead to a total run-time of:

$$T_c(A, B) = 2t_l + T(A) + t_{A_s} + t_{A_r} + max(t_{block}, t_l + T(B))$$

In this case, cooperative multitasking would reduce application run-time on slightly more relaxed conditions regarding $T(B)$:

$$T_c(A, B) < T_n(A, B) \Leftrightarrow \left\{ \begin{array}{l} t_{A_s} + t_{A_r} < T(B) \\ \wedge \quad t_l + t_{A_s} + t_{A_r} < t_{block} \end{array} \right.$$

However, because a hardware thread cannot first call a blocking function and then initiate a reconfiguration, the second mechanism would require integrating the hardware reconfiguration into the OS kernel's scheduler, which runs contradictory to the ReconOS goals of portability and transparency. The first approach can be implemented without kernel modifications using preemptively scheduled delegate and hardware scheduling threads, as detailed in Section 6.5.

It should be noted that the non-preemptive scheduling technique as outlined above is a special case of cooperative scheduling, in which the cooperating threads never yield. Thus, a poorly behaved cooperatively scheduled thread can make the system just as unresponsive as a non-preemptive one.

6.3.3 Experimental Evaluation

To evaluate the cooperative multitasking technique from Figure 6.1(c) and its associated overheads, we have run a range of benchmarks on a ReconOS prototype using the two threads A and B from the example in Section 6.3.2. Thread A with run time $T(A)$ calls a function which blocks for t_{block} until it returns. During this time, A yields the slot to B, which executes for $T(B)$ before reconfiguring and resuming A.

For the experiments, $T(A)$ and the reconfiguration time t_l have been fixed, while $T(B)$ and t_{block} have been varied from 0 to $5t_l$ and 0 to $9t_l$, respectively. For simplicity, t_{A_s} and t_{A_r} have been set to zero. The resulting performance gains compared to the non-preemptive technique are shown in Figure 6.2. As long as either $T(B)$ or t_{block} are shorter than the reconfiguration time t_l, cooperative multitasking executes slower than the sequential non-preemptive technique due to reconfiguration and scheduling overheads. If both parameters rise above t_l, the performance is determined by the relation between $T(B)$ and t_{block} and peaks when $T(B) = t_{block}$. This observation accurately reflects the argument of the previous section.

The involved absolute overheads of the different hardware thread scheduling operations are summarized in Section 7.2.3.

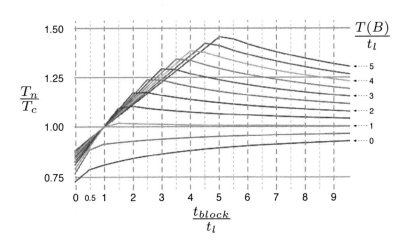

Figure 6.2: Performance of cooperative vs. non-preemptive multitasking. $T(B)$ and t_{block} are given relative to the reconfiguration time t_l.

hpt]

Call	Description
check_yield()	Checks for pending yield requests from the OS
flag_yield()	Marks the current OS call as 'yielding', and specifies the saved state encoding
thread_yield()	Relinquish control if there are waiting threads (to be used without other OS calls)
thread_resume()	Retrieves resume state information upon thread initialization to continue execution

Table 6.1: API functions for cooperative multitasking

6.4 Hardware Thread Modeling

In ReconOS, the cooperative scheduling technique is only employed for hardware threads contending for slots on the FPGA. Software threads are scheduled preemptively, according to their priorities, by the software scheduler of the host operating system.

The mechanisms for checking for waiting hardware threads and yielding execution are provided through the ReconOS VHDL API (Table 6.1). The state machine shown in Figure 6.3 is based on our previous example from Section 4.3.2 (page 54) and outlines an example of a hardware thread using these func-

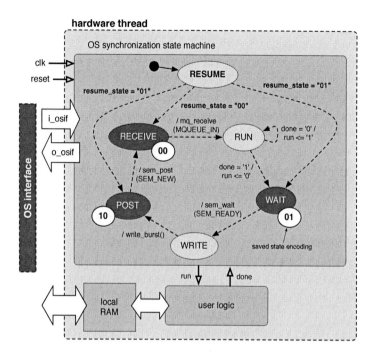

Figure 6.3: Cooperatively multithreading hardware thread. The thread starts
in a RESUME state and decides (based on an OS call) whether to
restart execution or to resume in a previous state. Dark states
denote possible points for yielding and are annotated with their
respective *resume state encoding*.

tions. The dark states in the OS synchronization state machine are potentially
yielding states, i.e. states which invoke blocking OS calls, during which the
hardware thread may be removed from the reconfigurable fabric until the OS
call returns.

Upon being loaded into a reconfigurable slot, a hardware thread cannot autonomously distinguish whether it has been started for the first time, or whether
it is supposed to resume execution in a state where it has previously yielded.
Therefore, the OS synchronization state machine always begins in the RE-
SUME state and executes a `reconos_thread_resume()` call. In the event that
the thread has been started for the first time, this call returns zero, causing
the state machine to transition to the regular first state (RECEIVE). Other-

Signal		Description
`yield`		Marks 'yielding' thread OS requests
`saved_state_enc`	$[0:log_2(n) - 1]$	Binary encoding of current thread FSM state (maximum n states)
`req_yield`		Indicates that other hardware threads are waiting for a slot

Table 6.2: OSIF communication signals for cooperative multitasking. Numbers in parenthesis denote signal widths.

wise, `reconos_thread_resume()` retrieves the saved state encoding as a *resume state encoding* and uses it to continue the state machine from the point of its previous interruption.

Should the hardware thread subsequently encounter a suitable state in which it can yield its slot, the corresponding OS call is augmented with a call to `flag_yield()`. This way, the hardware thread transmits a state encoding of its current state together with each yielding call to the OSIF and delegate thread, which saves it in the thread's kernel data structure as a *saved state encoding*. Now, during the flagged operating system call, the hardware thread can be replaced by the operating system, if other threads are waiting. As a consequence, a hardware thread must have its state saved to thread-local memory *before* flagging a call as yielding.

To prevent hardware threads from always saving their state before entering a yielding state where they might possibly be unloaded, ReconOS provides a dedicated signal indicating whether other threads waiting for a slot to become free. This flag can be read using the `check_yield()` function, which does not impose a timing overhead. Table 6.2 lists the corresponding signals added to the OSIF interface signals.

6.4.1 Creating and Terminating Multitasking Threads

We refer to the synthesized hardware circuit representing a specific thread's functionality as a *core*. For every available *slot* in the system, a hardware core is placed and routed, resulting in $n_{slots} \times n_{cores}$ partial *bitstreams*. There can be multiple hardware *thread* instantiations based on the same core. The data structures modeling the relationships between slots, hardware threads, cores and bitstreams are populated by the application designer and shared between the delegates and the hardware scheduler. As opposed to the creation of static hardware threads, as outlined in Section 4.5.1, dynamically hardware threads are not created with a static slot number attribute (set via

```
1  // include static bitstream arrays generated by bit2c
2  #include <prm0_routed_partial_bit.h>
3  #include <prm1_routed_partial_bit.h>
4  #include <prm2_routed_partial_bit.h>
5
6  // bitstreams
7  reconos_bitstream_t bitstream_0 = {
8      .slot_num = 0,
9      .data     = prm0_routed_partial_bit,
10     .size     = PRM0_ROUTED_PARTIAL_BIT_SIZE
11 };
12 reconos_bitstream_t bitstream_1 = {
13     .slot_num = 1,
14     .data     = prm1_routed_partial_bit,
15     .size     = PRM1_ROUTED_PARTIAL_BIT_SIZE
16 };
17 reconos_bitstream_t bitstream_2 = {
18     .slot_num = 2,
19     .data     = prm2_routed_partial_bit,
20     .size     = PRM2_ROUTED_PARTIAL_BIT_SIZE
21 };
22
23 // core
24 reconos_core_t my_core = {
25     .name       = "MY_CORE",
26     .bitstreams = {&bitstream_0, &bitstream_1, &bitstream_2},
27     .num_bitstreams = 3,
28     .signature = 0x12345678
29 };
30
31 // hardware thread object and attributes
32 rthread          hwthread;
33 pthread_attr_t  hwthread_swattr;
34 rthread_attr_t  hwthread_hwattr;
35
36 // initialization of hardware thread attributes
37 pthread_attr_init(&hwthread_swattr);
38 rthread_attr_init(&hwthread_hwattr);
39 rthread_attr_setcore(&hwthread_hwattr, &my_core);
40
41 // hardware thread creation
42 rthread_create(
43     &hwthread,                // thread object
44     &hwthread_swattr,         // software attributes
45     &hwthread_hwattr,         // hardware attributes
46     ( void * ) data           // entry data
47 );
```

Listing 6.1: Creation of partially reconfigurable hardware threads.

`rthreadattr_setslotnum()`), but are passed the data structures pertaining to the core representing the thread's functionality (via `rthreadattr_setcore()`). Also, dynamically reconfigurable and statically implemented hardware threads can be mixed within a ReconOS system.

Listing 6.1 shows an example of creating hardware threads suitable for partial reconfiguration, which can then either be scheduled cooperatively, or non-preemptively, depending on the actual hardware thread's behavior. Additionally to the software and hardware attributes required for static hardware threads (lines 33 and 34), the application designer needs to create data structures for the bitstreams (lines 7, 12, and 17) and cores (line 24), and reference them in the hardware thread's `rthread_attr` data structure (line 39) using `rthread_attr_setcore()`.

6.4.2 Context Saving and Restoring

Optimally, threads yield when they have minimal state information to be preserved across the period of being scheduled off the reconfigurable fabric. Whatever state information there is needs to be saved to main memory before yielding, and restored after resuming execution.

Identifying and storing the relevant state information is the task of the thread designer. ReconOS provides the thread-internal RAM, usually used for burst memory transactions, as a close and easy to access intermediate storage for state information, which is automatically saved and restored on reconfiguration by the operating system kernel.

Although access to the local memory is fast and comparably simple, it still incurs an overhead (see Section 7.2.3). To avoid saving state information unnecessarily, a hardware thread can use the `check_yield()` API function to check for pending yield requests, and only save its state if it is about to be removed.

6.5 OS integration

The task of managing the reconfigurable resources in ReconOS is shared between a hardware thread's *delegate thread* and a high-priority software thread, the *hardware scheduler*, both of which are managed by the OS' preemptive scheduler. This approach provides excellent portability, since it does not involve any changes to the underlying software operating system's kernel.

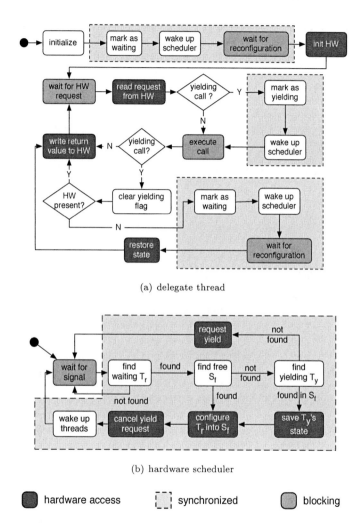

(a) delegate thread

(b) hardware scheduler

hardware access   synchronized   blocking

Figure 6.4: Control flow of delegate threads and the hardware scheduler. The areas marked as *synchronized* are protected by a scheduling mutex.

Figure 6.4 shows the control flow diagrams for both the delegate thread and the hardware scheduler. Upon invocation, the hardware scheduler (Figure 6.4(b)) checks all hardware threads' and slots' scheduling information. For any hardware thread waiting for execution, it looks for a slot—free or possibly with a yielding thread in it—to reconfigure it into. In the event that there are no free slots, the scheduler sends a request to yield to all running threads. This request causes the `check_yield()` API function to return `True`, which allows hardware threads to easily check for other hardware threads waiting to be executed, avoiding unnecessary saving of state information. If a hardware thread is newly started, its delegate (Figure 6.4(a)) requests its associated hardware core to be loaded by setting a flag in its scheduling data structure and notifying the hardware scheduler. After the corresponding partial bitstream has been configured to the FPGA, the delegate continues waiting for and serving OS call requests from the hardware. If any of these calls carries a 'yielding' flag set by the hardware, the thread notes this in its scheduling data structure and notifies the scheduler. Upon completion of such a call, this flag is again cleared. Should the thread's hardware core have been replaced during the call, the delegate thread requests the reloading of its core and wakes up the scheduler. After reconfiguration, the hardware thread's state is restored and normal execution resumes.

As the software threads run in a preemptive environment, it is necessary to protect the shared data structures through the use of a mutex (shown as dashed boxes in Figure 6.4). Also, as accesses to the hardware (e.g., for reading call parameters or writing yield requests) are non-atomic, they too need to be synchronized on a per-slot basis (shown as dark processes).

6.5.1 Cooperative Scheduling in a Preemptive Environment

By applying the concept of delegate threads introduced in Section 3.3.3, co-operatively scheduled hardware threads must rely on preemptively scheduled software threads for their operation. Thus, in the ReconOS environment, the concepts of cooperative and preemptive scheduling must be combined, and special care must be taken not to introduce deadlocks or reduce the utilization of resources.

On a sequentially scheduled preemptive system with multiple priority levels, the execution order of threads is determined by a priority assigned to the individual thread. When more than one thread is ready to run (i.e., not blocking on a resource), the one with the higher priority is selected. This scheme generally controls the order in which multiple threads competing for a single resource are granted access, not only regarding processing elements (i.e., the CPU or a slot), but also resources like semaphore, message queues, or mutexes. In other words, a thread with a high priority is regarded as more important than a thread with a lower priority, and is consequently granted processing time when needed.

Introducing heterogeneous multiprocessing systems, such as ReconOS, raises additional issues, both pertaining to its heterogeneity as well as to its cooperatively (or non-preemptively) scheduled nature. A non-negligible efficiency issue involving our heterogeneous approach is independent from the fact that hardware threads are not preemptible at arbitrary times. It occurs even when there are as many or more slots available than runnable hardware threads. If we assign a hardware thread's delegate a priority in line with the thread's importance among its software peers, a higher-priority software thread might block the execution of this delegate, even if it would only execute a simple, non-blocking OS call. While this behavior is appropriate with respect to the access order to arbitrary resources, it effectively prevents the associated reconfigurable hardware area to be idle, even if it had data to process. This issue is not a violation of the underlying scheduling principle—after all, the software thread *is* more important than the hardware thread—, but it is an issue that lowers the system's performance, which is in contrast with the goals of integrating hardware threads in the first place. Moreover, this issue is singular to a heterogeneous parallel system such as ReconOS; in a single-processor scenario, the lower-priority thread could not run anyway, since there are no free execution units, while in a traditional multi-processor system, the OS call would be executed in kernel space, which supersedes the priorities of all running software threads.

To avoid this efficiency issue, we generally raise the priority of a delegate thread above the priorities of all other software threads. As the operations executed within the delegate thread are either very short or result in a blocking OS call, the CPU is released within a very short time after an incoming OS call from hardware. This approach ensures that the hardware processing resources do not remain unnecessarily idle, while not imposing unreasonable delays on the software portions of an application.

However, there is a distinct disadvantage associated with this technique. The high priority of a delegate thread will give it a general precedence when competing with other threads for resources, such as a message queue. This applies especially for systems designed in a farming pattern—shown in Figure 6.5—, where several worker threads are fed data through a single mailbox or message queue. In this setting, a hardware thread will more often process messages than its software peers. This is generally not a problem, since a specialized hardware thread typically exhibits more processing performance than a func-

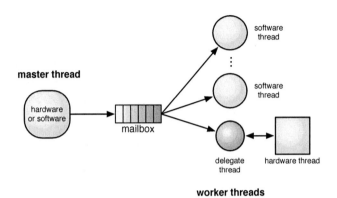

Figure 6.5: Example of a farming pattern with software and hardware threads as workers. Access arbitration to the mailbox is controlled by the thread's priorities.

tionally equivalent software thread. When cooperatively scheduling hardware threads, however, a high-priority delegate thread may retrieve a message (or any other resource), even while its associated hardware thread is not present within the reconfigurable fabric. The hardware thread will not be able to process the message until a slot becomes free, which is not controlled by priorities, but by the cooperative behavior of other hardware threads. Even more significantly, since the message has already been retrieved by the delegate, other runnable software threads have no chance to process the message, even if their processing resource is available.

The sequence diagram in Figure 6.6 illustrates this problem. At the beginning, both a software thread (bearing a priority of 5) and hardware thread, represented by its delegate (bearing a higher priority of 7), are blocking on a `mbox_get()` OS call, because the corresponding mailbox is empty. Since the hardware thread is inactive during this blocking period, it yields its slot to another thread, and is removed from the reconfigurable fabric. Shortly after, a message appears in the mailbox, causing the delegate thread to wake up due to its higher priority compared to the software thread. It retrieves the message from the mailbox, but is unable to relay it to its hardware thread, which is presently not loaded onto the FPGA. Thus, a period of inactivity ensues, in which the hardware thread holds a message that could have been better served by handing it over to the software thread. Only when a slot becomes free (due to some other thread yielding or terminating), the message can be processed by the hardware thread.

In a sense, this problem appears because the processing of such a thread is distributed among two separate processing resources (a slot for the hardware thread and the CPU for its delegate), of which one is available and the other is not. Consequently, we apply a priority policy which avoids this issue by lowering the priority of the delegate thread's priority below that of all other software threads while its hardware is not present and there are no free slots. In this way, the embattled resource will not be claimed by the delegate, but by any other waiting software threads, until a slot becomes available.

The new sequence of events under this priority policy is depicted in Figure 6.7. Here, under the same starting conditions as in Figure 6.6, the delegate thread's priority is set to 3 as soon as its hardware thread is removed. This causes the software thread—now being of a higher priority—to retrieve the arriving message from the mailbox. The delegate's priority is restored at the moment a slot becomes available (again, due to some other thread yielding or terminating), allowing the delegate thread to preempt the still processing software thread to quickly serve the next `mbox_get()` request for its hardware.

This policy results in three disjunct blocks of assignable priorities in the system. $P_{HW,running}$, containing all delegates with running and runnable hardware threads, P_{SW}, which are the (fixed) priorities of all regular software threads in the system, and $P_{HW,non-present}$, for all delegates whose hardware threads are currently not configured (nor currently configurable) to the FPGA. The order within the blocks preserves the order of the priorities assigned at thread creation, so that the application designer can use the same priorities for calls to `pthread_create()` and `rthread_create()`. The actual priority p of a delegate as used by the scheduler is determined as follows:

$$p = \begin{cases} p_{assigned} + (max(P_{SW}) - min(P_{SW})) & \text{if HW present or free slots} \\ p_{assigned} - (max(P_{SW}) - min(P_{SW})) & \text{if HW not present, no free slots} \end{cases}$$

$p_{assigned}$ is the 'regular' priority assigned to the hardware thread on thread creation, with $min(P_{SW}) \leq p_{assigned} \leq max(P_{SW})$.

6.6 Tool Integration

We have integrated the described methods for non-preemptive and cooperative multitasking into the ReconOS tool chain presented in Section 5.2. This involves both extensions of the ReconOS hardware synthesis process, as well

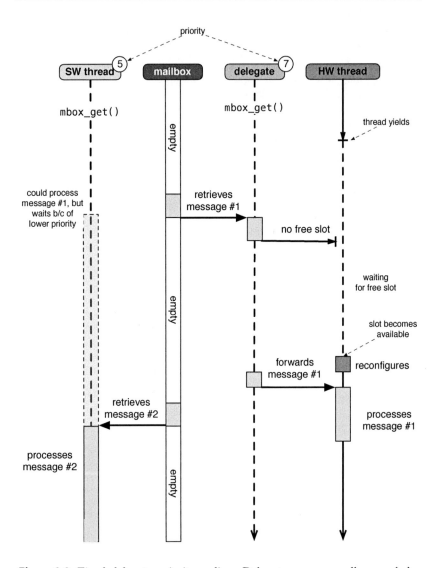

Figure 6.6: Fixed delegate priority policy. Delegates are generally awarded a higher priority than regular software threads to speed up hardware OS request processing. This can lead to underutilization of the CPU.

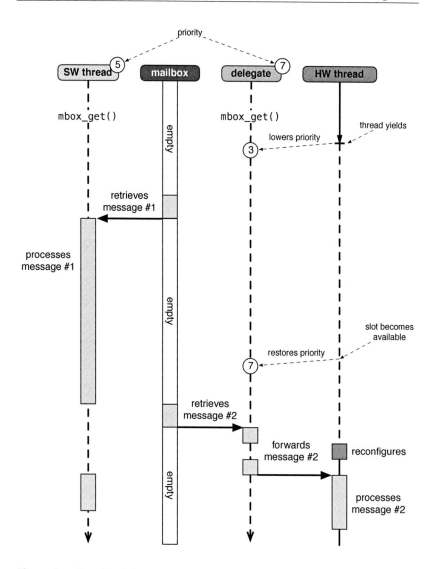

Figure 6.7: Variable delegate priority policy. Delegates only gain a high priority when their hardware thread is present or can be reconfigured. This prevents delegates from retrieving messages without being able to handle them.

as integration of the partially reconfigurable bitstreams into the software executable.

6.6.1 Hardware

We have extended the ReconOS tool chain for bitstream generation, as introduced in Section 5.2.1, to support the automatic generation of a partially reconfigurable system. The only changes visible to the designer involve information about static and dynamic threads, and the physical layout of the reconfigurable slots. The thread-related information specifies which hardware threads are to be statically synthesized into the fixed portion of the design, and which hardware threads are to be generated as partially reconfigurable bitstreams. This data is provided to the tools via the ReconOS project file using the STATIC_THREADS and DYNAMIC_THREADS definitions (see Appendix A.4). The physical layout is provided using a dedicated description file that specifies the exact shape and location of the individual slots that make up the dynamically reconfigurable area of the targeted FPGA. This *layout* file lists the area constraints and bus macro locations of the design (see Appendix A.3). The remaining area not occupied by the slots from the layout file is automatically allocated for placement of the static components of the system.

System Assembly

Starting from the same reference design as a static design, the tool chain inserts the following infrastructure components necessary for partial reconfiguration:

Bus macros: In a partially reconfigurable design built according to the modular tool flow proposed by Xilinx [117], all dynamically reconfigurable logic modules are synthesized, placed, and routed together with the static part, but independently from the other dynamic modules. Consequently, given the differences between the dynamic modules and the nondeterministic nature of the placement and routing algorithms, it is possible that the signals crossing the boundary between the statically configured part of the design—in our case the OSIF—and the dynamically reconfigurable area—the slots—are routed using different resources of FPGA's interconnection network. To ensure that all dynamic modules are compatible with the static part, these signals need to be fixed to pre-specified locations on the chip using dedicated logic, the *bus macros*. The tool chain determines the number of necessary bus macros from the system's VHDL description, inserts them into the top level design,and creates the necessary constraint files for the implementation tools based on the specified layout file. All bus macros routing output signals from the hardware thread feature an enable input, which is connected to the associated OSIF. Upon dynamically reconfiguring a hardware thread, its outputs are disabled using this signal in order to ensure that possible glitches on the outputs during writing of the partial bitstream do not interfere with the OSIF's operation.

Clock routing: The Xilinx partial reconfiguration tool flow requires that all global clock networks used by a system need to be routed through clock buffers (BUFGs) on the top level of the design. Thus, it is necessary to modify the base reference design and extract all BUFGs from their modules onto the top level. In ReconOS, this is done by creating dedicated `clock_logic` IP cores that contain only BUFGs, and using them explicitly instead of inferring the clock buffers automatically within the digital clock managers (DCMs) of the system. These `clock_logic` cores are replaced with BUFG primitives during the assembly of the partially reconfigurable system, and corresponding constraints added to the design.

Figure 6.8 shows the complete hardware tool flow for the partially reconfigurable ReconOS system. For the static part of the system, the tool flow differs from the static one described in Figure 5.6 (page 87) only in adding the necessary bus macro infrastructure for partial reconfiguration. In fact, it is possible to generate a purely static implementation of a system including the additional bus macro logic for timing analysis. For a complete dynamically reconfigurable system, all dynamic hardware threads are synthesized, placed, and routed independently and then merged with the static design using the Xilinx early-access partial reconfiguration (EAPR) tools. This results in a full bitstream for the static part of the design and several partial bitstreams for all dynamic thread/slot combinations.

6.6.2 Software

The software necessary for controlling the reconfiguration process—in particular the hardware scheduler and the additional delegate thread code to communicate with it—is integrated in the ReconOS operating system package. Corresponding entries in the eCos configuration framework ensure that these routines are only included into systems explicitly configured for partial reconfiguration.

The partial bitstreams for reconfiguring the individual cores into the system's slots need to be stored in main memory prior to the activation of the dy-

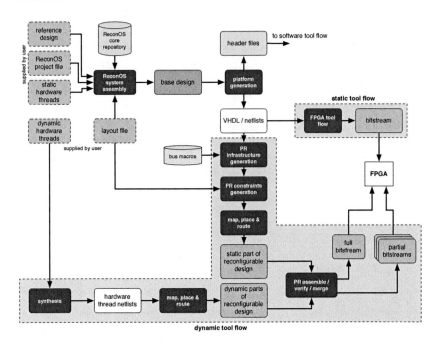

Figure 6.8: ReconOS hardware tool flow for partially reconfigurable systems. Dynamic hardware threads are processed into partial bitstreams, while static threads and the ReconOS infrastructure are assembled into a full bitstream. Dark boxes denote processes performed by ReconOS or Xilinx EAPR tools.

namic hardware threads. Usually, within our prototype implementations, this is achieved by linking them as static and constant C arrays into the global data segment of the application's software executable. Conversion between partial bit files (*.bit) and compilable and linkable C files (*.c/*.h) is done by a custom *bit2c* tool integrated into the software tool chain. Figure 6.9 shows the complete software eCos tool flow for an application including partially reconfigurable hardware threads.

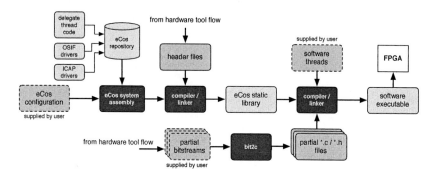

Figure 6.9: ReconOS software tool flow for partially reconfigurable systems. Partial bitstreams are integrated into the application's software executable. Dark boxes denote processes performed by ReconOS or the regular compiler tool chain.

6.7 Chapter Conclusion

In this chapter we have presented hardware multitasking as a method to time-share an FPGA's reconfigurable resources between processing elements. ReconOS transparently supports hardware multitasking through the dynamic reconfiguration of hardware threads. It offers two multitasking models: *non-preemptive* multitasking, where hardware threads run uninterrupted from creation to completion, and *cooperative* multitasking, which allows the preemption of hardware threads at specified preemption points, usually during blocking operating system calls.

Compared to non-preemptive multitasking, the cooperative approach has the potential of better area utilization, as inactive hardware threads can be temporarily replaced by other runnable hardware threads. At the same time, this increases the number of reconfigurations, causing the total reconfiguration overhead to rise. As a result, the two techniques are applicable to different scenarios. Applications which are able to tolerate reconfiguration delays or require only infrequent repartitioning can improve their area utilization by cooperatively sharing the reconfigurable resources. Other applications can still benefit from run-time reconfiguration by utilizing the non-preemptive approach. Reducing reconfiguration overheads is a major focus of ongoing efforts to improve the reconfiguration infrastructure of FPGA-based systems, and will increase the number of applicable scenarios for cooperative hardware multitasking.

In the next chapter, the concepts of ReconOS will be applied to real-world applications and prototypes to quantify overheads and demonstrate the feasibility of our approach.

CHAPTER 7

Experimental Results

This chapter presents prototype implementations of the ReconOS execution platform. The performance figures derived from these prototypes are intended to provide the quantitative foundations for selecting the most suitable OS service implementation for a given problem. We quantify individual overheads and performance characteristics of the OS services provided by ReconOS, and, using application case studies for illustration, show how the development concepts and advantages of our proposed programming and execution models can be applied to real-world examples.

During the course of the ReconOS project, several application case studies have been created to evaluate and demonstrate different capabilities of the ReconOS execution environment and their applicability to different problem domains:

Image processing: Reisch developed a multithreaded image processing library [90] akin to the the software library supplied with Texas Instruments DSPs; Happe implemented a on-line visual object-tracking application based on a sequential Monte-Carlo simulation framework [8, 9, 48] (see also Section 7.3.3); together with Angermeier and Rullmann, we showed a demonstrator for high-level-synthesis based image processing threads [4].

Cryptography: Wildenhain implemented a multithreaded stream encryption application [111] incorporating the Blowfish and RC5 algorithms.

Communication Systems: Agne developed an adaptive[1] Huffman encoder within multithreaded hardware; together with Keller, we employed ReconOS for augmenting adaptive networking methods [62] with reconfigurable hardware support.

We have selected three representative applications to be described in detail in Section 7.3. While these applications are not intended to present the most effective implementations of their respective algorithms, they serve to illustrate how the concepts presented in previous chapters can be applied to real-world problems and applications. All case studies presented in this chapter have been created using the ReconOS tool flow outlined in Chapter 5; thus, they also show that the tool flow and associated development techniques can handle real-world examples.

Section 7.1 will introduce the three basic execution platforms serving as a basis for the remaining parts of the chapter. The overheads and performance figures extracted from benchmarks on these platforms are presented and summarized in Section 7.2. Section 7.3 presents more elaborate case studies demonstrating ReconOS' design objectives.

7.1 Prototype Platforms

Based on the hardware architecture shown in Figure 3.6 (p. 44) and the two OS kernels presented in Section 5.1 (p. 77), we have created three ReconOS prototype platforms: *ReconOS / eCos-PPC*, *ReconOS / Linux-PPC*, and *ReconOS / Linux-MicroBlaze*. The main features of these prototypes are listed in Table 7.1. The memory and control buses are realized with CoreConnect PLB and DCR buses, respectively. External SDRAM is used for both the operating system and shared thread memory. The prototypes also include I/O peripherals, such as serial ports, Ethernet interfaces, and general-purpose-I/O, all of which are managed by the software operating system kernel. Both the OS interfaces and the hardware threads run at the system's bus clock, which is 100 MHz for all prototypes.

The software parts of the first two prototypes executes on the FPGA's embedded PowerPC 405 running at 300 MHz, while the third prototype runs a noMMU variant of Linux on a MicroBlaze v4.0 soft core processor clocked at 100 MHz. Both Linux systems run a 2.6 kernel.

---

[1]Here, the term *adaptive* covers both the on-line generation of the Huffman codebook, as well as using reconfigurable hardware threads for the encoder's implementation.

| | Prototype (ReconOS/−) | | |
	eCos-PPC	Linux-PPC	Linux-MicroBlaze
Operating system	eCos	Linux	Linux
Based on kernel	eCos-VIRTEX4 [79]	2.6-virtex [95]	2.6-nommu [88]
CPU	PowerPC 405	PowerPC 405	MicroBlaze 4.0
FPGA	XC2VP30 / XC4VFX100	XC2VP30	XC4VSX35
CPU clock	300 MHz	300 MHz	100 MHz
PLB/DCR bus clock	100 MHz	100 MHz	100 MHz
MMU	no	yes	no

Table 7.1: ReconOS prototype platforms.

7.2 Performance and Overheads

Introducing a layer of abstraction often comes at the cost of performance. It is the task of the system's designer to decide on a reasonable trade-off between conflicting properties when selecting a run-time environment and associated development model for a given application. In the following, we present raw overheads and performance numbers based on measurements taken from synthetic benchmark applications run on the previously introduced prototypes.

7.2.1 Area

A complete OS interface requires about 1738 slices which amount to 12.7 % / 11.3 % / 4.1 % of the logic resources of the employed XC2VP30, XC4VSX35 and XC4VFX100 FPGAs, respectively. The largest contributor to the OSIF's area consumption are the virtual memory management subsystem and the PLB bus interface, both of which take up over a third of the OS interface's slice requirements. Most of the remaining logic is used for the command decoder and the DCR bus interface. An OSIF for systems without virtual memory management, for example ReconOS/eCos, requires 1040 slices (7.6 % / 6.8 % / 2.5 %). Configuring an OSIF for minimal resource consumption by removing the PLB interface and the HWT-MMU results in a total area of about 420 slices (3.1 % / 2.7 % / 1.0 %). Table 7.2 shows synthesis estimates of the individual area requirements of the OSIF's modules in slices, look-up tables, flip-flops and BRAMs[2].

The interface between an OSIF and a hardware thread requires 47 `osif2task` and 51 `task2osif` signals, plus 151 signals for accessing the thread-local RAM.

---

[2]Note that possible cross-module optimizations when synthesizing a complete OSIF may reduce the total area requirements below the sum of the individual components.

Component	Slices	LUTs	FFs	BRAMs
OSIF	1738	3043	1430	3
PLB I/F	691	713	259	0
HWT-MMU	370	622	323	0
TLB	328	598	299	3
Command decoder	307	547	199	0
DCR I/F	86	151	76	0

Table 7.2: OSIF resource utilization.

In a partially reconfigurable ReconOS system, this amounts to 32 8-bit bus-macros occupying an additional 256 slices per slot, half of which lie in the static and dynamic area, respectively.

Adding support for cooperative multitasking to a hardware thread will increase the amount of states in the thread's OS FSM, and may also introduce additional logic for storing context in the the thread-local RAM. The amount of area overhead incurred by these mechanisms are highly thread-specific and can thus not be generally quantified. However, as most threads already incorporate logic for accessing the thread-local RAM as a result of their regular processing tasks, the saving and restoring of thread state can re-use this logic without introducing a significant overhead.

7.2.2 Operating System Calls

The first set of experiments employs a set of synthetic threads analyzing the performance of timing critical OS calls. The mutex and semaphore primitives from Table 4.2 (p. 58) serve as representative examples, as most other supported API calls are either based on them or are not considered timing critical.

The threads measure the raw execution time of single API calls to lock (unlock) a mutex or post (wait for) a semaphore, respectively, as well as a measure we call the *turnaround time*. The turnaround time is defined as the time it takes from one thread releasing a mutex (posting a semaphore), to the next thread acquiring a lock (receiving the semaphore). The experiments have been run with different combinations of software and hardware threads. The results are shown in Table 7.3.

Synchronization operations on the eCos kernel behave as expected: calls from hardware are more expensive than their software counterparts due to the additional interrupt processing and hardware accesses. The Linux implementations show a similar behavior but differ in certain details. Overall, OS calls are sig-

	Bus cycles (10 ns)		
	eCos/PPC	Linux/PPC	Linux/MicroBlaze
Mutex (raw OS calls)			
SW lock	83	821	9178
SW unlock	171	551	9179
HW lock	959	7769	35855
HW unlock	679	2636	22360
Mutex (turnaround)			
SW → SW	453	8821	83657
SW → HW	629	9824	90515
HW → SW	1449	14371	121673
HW → HW	1460	14102	126668
Semaphore (raw OS calls)			
SW post	73	598	13180
HW post	695	1972	22116
Semaphore (turnaround)			
SW → SW	305	9094	203221
SW → HW	528	9575	207824
HW → SW	908	12291	145924
HW → HW	1114	12196	154013

Table 7.3: Performance of ReconOS synchronization primitives.

nificantly more expensive in a Linux kernel than in eCos; a fact which can be attributed to context switches to and from kernel mode when executing OS functions. On a PowerPC CPU running at the same speed, the Linux calls take about an order of magnitude longer than the corresponding eCos calls. Using a considerably less powerful MicroBlaze soft core processor clocked at a third of the clock frequency, the execution times rise by another order of magnitude.

7.2.3 Hardware Scheduling

To evaluate the cooperative scheduling technique and to obtain quantitative measurements on the involved overheads, we have implemented a prototype system executing cooperating thread sets with varying parameters (see Section 6.3.3). We have measured the timing overheads of individual operations, such as the saving and restoring of state information, scheduling operations and also the configuration overhead.

---

[1] This large delay can be attributed to the usage of the Xilinx OPB HWICAP configuration core. By using improved interfaces [28], we expect that this time could be cut by more than an order of magnitude, resulting in a configuration time of under 5 ms.

Thread operation	Bus cycles (10 ns)
check_yield()	0
flag_yield()	0
thread_yield() (no thread waiting)	4
thread_yield() (threads waiting)	700
thread_resume()	4
Store/load state to/from local RAM (32 bit)	1
Store state directly to main memory (32 bit)	26
Load state directly from main memory (32 bit)	32

OS operation	Duration / throughput
Thread initialization	1.76 ms
Thread suspend	93.12 μs
Thread resume	192.32 μs
State save (4096 bytes)	37.51 μs (104.1 MB/s)
State restore (4096 bytes)	45.19 μs (86.4 MB/s)
Reconfiguration time (233 kBytes)	99,96 ms [1]

Table 7.4: Execution times of thread and OS operations.

The prototype employs a ReconOS/eCos-PPC operating system on a XCV2P30 FPGA platform using a single reconfigurable slot and operating frequencies of 300 MHz and 100 MHz for the CPU and the reconfigurable logic, respectively. Table 7.4 shows the execution times of individual operations that can be invoked by the hardware thread, as well the overheads of thread control, state save/restore and reconfiguration operations performed by the operating system.

check_yield() and flag_yield() are concurrent signal comparisons and assignments which do not require separate state machine cycles. thread_yield() will only suspend the thread's operation when there are other threads waiting; this involves an interrupt of the CPU. If there are no waiting hardware threads, it takes 4 cycles to return, which is the handshake latency of the OS synchronization state machine. Transferring data from the hardware thread to thread-local RAM can be done with 32 bits per clock cycle; this data then needs to be stored/loaded to/from main memory by the delegate thread. Alternatively, a thread can transfer single 32 bit values directly from or to main memory.

The results show that the overhead incurred by the scheduling API remains acceptably small, particularly in the event that no other hardware thread is waiting for a slot. Thus, augmenting a hardware thread with cooperative scheduling operations will not have a significant impact on the performance of the thread itself. However, the reconfiguration process itself is by far the most expensive operation. For the reconfigurable regions (13 × 17 CLBs) used in our prototype, which require partial bitstreams of 233 kBytes each, the reconfigu-

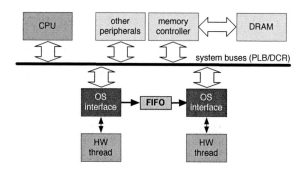

Figure 7.1: Hardware architecture with a thread-to-thread FIFO.

ration time dwarfs any memory accesses for state saving or restoring. While this time can be reduced by more than an order of magnitude by improving the configuration port interface core [28] or by minimizing the bitstream size [28][94], it remains a limiting factor that determines what applications can be feasibly implemented with any hardware multitasking technique.

7.2.4 Communication

In a further experiment, we have analyzed the attainable throughput for the communication primitives available to ReconOS threads. Two threads perform a sequence of data transfers, subsequently reading and writing data from and to main memory, as well as reading and writing data from and to mailboxes and message queues. Several configurations of the test have been run, using hardware and software threads, and with mailboxes mapped either to hardware FIFOs or to eCos software mailboxes. The throughput of ReconOS communication primitives for hardware threads depends primarily on the specifics of the hardware architecture (e.g. memory bus width and frequency), which is identical for the ReconOS/eCos and ReconOS/Linux prototypes. For this test, the ReconOS/eCos prototype employing a PowerPC processor was selected.

Figure 7.1 shows the architecture used for testing the configuration with two hardware threads and a hardware FIFO. The first hardware thread reads 8 kBytes of data from main memory into its local RAM. It then uses the ReconOS mailbox calls to transfer this data to the hardware FIFO, one 32-bit word at a time. Simultaneously, the second hardware thread reads from the hardware FIFO, also by using the ReconOS mailbox API. Once this data transfer is completed, the second thread writes the data back to main memory.

	With data cache		Without data cache	
Operation	**[μs]**	**[MB/s]**	**[μs]**	**[MB/s]**
MEM→HW (burst read)	45.74	170.80	46.41	168.34
HW→MEM (burst write)	40.54	192.71	40.55	192.66
MEM→SW→MEM (memcpy)	132.51	58.96	625.00	12.50
HW→HW (mailbox)	61.42	127.20	61.42	127.20
SW→HW (mailbox)	58500	0.13	374000	0.02
HW→SW (mailbox)	58510	0.13	374000	0.02
SW→HW (message queue)	472.00	16.55	2166.79	3.61
HW→SW (message queue)	482.31	16.20	2160.69	3.62

Table 7.5: Performance of ReconOS communication primitives. All operations were run for 8 kBytes of data.

The hardware FIFOs are implemented as parametrizable IP cores that can be easily instantiated and connected via the Xilinx EDK or by the ReconOS build system. To transfer one word of data to or from a FIFO, a hardware thread needs three cycles. This includes all handshaking between hardware thread and the OSIF's command decoder as well as between the OSIF's FIFO manager and the FIFO core. The additional FIFO manager increases the OSIF's area requirements only by 64 slices or 5%.

During the experiment, we have measured the times for reading and writing the data from and to main memory, and the times for writing and reading the data to and from the mailboxes. For comparison, we have also measured the times for data transfer between hardware and software threads using ReconOS' message queue primitives. Since software threads do not possess local memory, the memory read/write tests for software threads have been combined into a single *memcopy* test. The results are shown in Table 7.5.

While the hardware FIFOs only achieve 66% to 74% of the memory bus (PLB) in terms of raw throughput, one has to keep in mind that in order to transfer data from one thread to another, two memory transactions have to occur: first, the sending thread needs to write to shared memory, before the receiving thread can read the data. When using hardware FIFOs, reading and writing can occur concurrently. Considering this, an 8 kByte data transfer via hardware FIFOs is about 40% faster than a transfer of the same data via shared memory. Also, the transfer via mailboxes is implicitly synchronized, while two threads exchanging data via shared memory need explicit synchronization, e.g., via mutexes or semaphores.

The above figures show that for applications able to chain several hardware threads together for data processing, the hardware FIFOs provide improved performance and reduced bus load over shared memory. Importantly, hardware

FIFOs fully maintain transparency and flexibility using the ReconOS programming model abstractions. Mailbox-based data transfers across the hardware/-software boundary use regular eCos software mailboxes with data structures located in shared memory. Due to the overheads involved with relaying OS calls from hardware to the CPU, mailbox-based data transfer between hardware and software threads is rather inefficient. On the other hand, direct shared memory communication with several orders of magnitude better performance comes at the cost of explicit synchronization and cache coherency issues. A compromise between transparency and performance is established by the ReconOS message queue primitives, which map directly to POSIX message queues and hide the details of shared memory access and explicit cache management from the user. As expected, their achievable data throughput performance lies between that of direct memory access and software mailboxes.

In a virtual memory environment, such as Linux, memory accesses from a hardware thread are translated into physical addresses by the HWT-MMU integrated into the OSIF. This involves additional delays for TLB look-ups or, in case of a TLB miss, for retrieving address mappings from the page tables stored in main memory. The resulting latencies gathered during experiments for single and burst transfers, as well as the delays caused by page faults, are listed in Table 7.6. Compared to the case without address translation, memory accesses to addresses already cached in the TLB increase by 4.7% to 17.4%. On a TLB miss, the HWT-MMU needs to perform a page table walk, which adds between 87% and 374% of latency. Finally, page faults are deferred to the delegate thread and incur the expected interrupt processing and context switching overhead of more than a millisecond.

	Condition		
Access type	**TLB hit**	**TLB miss**	**Page fault**
Single word			
Read	$0.50\mu s$ $(+\ 8.7\%)$	$1.22\mu s$ $(+165\%)$	$1314\mu s$
Write	$0.27\mu s$ $(+\ 17.4\%)$	$1.09\mu s$ $(+374\%)$	$1293\mu s$
Burst			
Read	$0.89\mu s$ $(+\ 4.7\%)$	$1.59\mu s$ $(+87\%)$	$1324\mu s$
Write	$0.63\mu s$ $(+\ 6.8\%)$	$1.35\mu s$ $(+129\%)$	$1301\mu s$

Table 7.6: Latencies caused by address translations of the HWT-MMU for single word and burst accesses. 1 bus cycle = 10 ns.

7.2.5 Discussion

While the increased flexibility afforded by the software-based implementation of operating system services comes with a considerable overhead, we argue that for the case of reconfigurable hardware accelerators modeled as threads, typical applications will not see a substantial performance hit. Generally, the somewhat limited reconfigurable area will be used to speed up highly data-parallel tasks requiring relatively few OS interactions for synchronization, while control-dominated tasks are more likely to be implemented as a software-thread executed by the system's CPU, where the overhead associated with OS calls is significantly lower. Additionally, the dedicated memory interfaces for hardware threads are usually more efficient in servicing regular access patterns for data-centric computations, e.g., streaming. This reasonable partitioning between control- and data-centric processing is also evident in the application case studies of the following section.

7.3 Examples and Case Studies

We have implemented several more elaborate application case studies using ReconOS prototype platforms. In the following, we will present a selection of applications to demonstrate the design approach and benefits of our proposed programming model and execution platforms in a more complex setting:

- An image processing application utilizing incremental design and legacy components to quickly generate a prototype and successively improve the system's performance

- A sorting application showing the portability of ReconOS applications across different target platforms and host operating systems

- A framework for dynamic state tracking using sequential Monte-Carlo methods demonstrating flexible design space exploration and applying the dynamic reconfiguration capabilities for data-dependent run-time adaption of the HW/SW partitioning

7.3.1 Image Processing

Our first application running on the ReconOS/eCos prototype demonstrates the iterative design approach made possible by the multithreaded programming model. In this application, grayscale image data is acquired from a web cam and streamed into the embedded target system through Ethernet, using

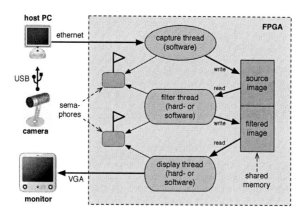

Figure 7.2: Image processing application. Image data is streamed via Ethernet from a host PC. Three threads (*capture, filter,* and *display*) process the data before displaying the result on an external monitor.

a TCP/IP stack running on eCos. The image data is then run through a convolution filter (in this case, a $w \times w$ Laplacian edge detection kernel), and subsequently copied to a frame buffer for display on an external monitor. The application consists of three threads: a capture, a filter and a display thread, as depicted in Figure 7.2. Data is passed between the threads through shared memory, while semaphores synchronize access to the memory.

The application was first implemented and tested purely in software, where all three threads are scheduled in sequence, as shown in Figure 7.3(a). Then, as a first try at optimization, we have coded the Laplacian in VHDL and turned it into a hardware thread. Convolution filters are amenable to parallelization which promises a considerable performance boost if the filter thread is moved to hardware.

Table 7.7 lists the execution times in ms per frame for the different threads and Laplacian kernel sizes, excluding any overhead due to OS calls. It can be seen that the hardware filter thread outperforms its software counterpart by a factor of 3.98 and 11.42 for a 3×3 and 5×5 kernel, respectively. If we execute all three threads in sequence, as shown in Figure 7.3(b), the theoretical speedup for this configuration amounts to 1.4 for a 3×3 filter, and 2.7 for a 5×5 filter. In practice, these speedups will not be reached due to the overhead of the OS.

Although, at this point, the application utilizes the FPGAs fine-grained parallelism by performing the convolution filter in hardware, the potential of thread-

Thread	Execution time [ms/frame]	
	Software	Hardware
Capture	16.0	—
Filter 3×3	23.9	6.0
Filter 5×5	86.6	7.6
Display	22.5	3.1

Table 7.7: Raw execution times of the image processing threads.

w	Configuration		Block size [image lines]				
			4	8	20	40	80
3	SW-SW-SW	(a)	14.4 (1.00)	15.5 (1.00)	16.1 (1.00)	16.2 (1.00)	16.3 (1.00)
	SW-HW-SW	(b)	15.5 (1.08)	17.6 (1.14)	18.6 (1.16)	**19.0 (1.17)**	18.9 (1.16)
	SW-HW-HW	(c)				23.5 (1.45)	23.4 (1.44)
	SW-HW-HW*	(d)				25.5 (1.57)	25.2 (1.55)
5	SW-SW-SW	(a)	8.1 (1.00)	8.3 (1.00)	8.5 (1.00)	8.5 (1.00)	8.5 (1.00)
	SW-HW-SW	(b)	15.3 (1.89)	17.0 (2.05)	18.4 (2.16)	**18.6 (2.19)**	18.6 (2.19)
	SW-HW-HW	(c)				23.2 (2.73)	23.0 (2.71)
	SW-HW-HW*	(d)				25.4 (2.99)	25.1 (2.95)

Table 7.8: Image processing system throughput for different configurations. Figures in parenthesis denote relative speedups.

level parallelism is not yet exploited. Therefore, the next optimization step has been to implement the display thread, which post-processes the filtered image for display, in hardware. Because the display and capture threads can now be run in different execution contexts (CPU and FPGA), they do not have to be executed in sequence anymore, which is shown in Figure 7.3(c). To further improve the thread-level parallelism, double buffering of the image data has been introduced. This allows all three threads to run simultaneously and is depicted in Figure 7.3(d).

The image processing application has been run with differently sized blocks of data. Larger block sizes reduce the system call overhead for semaphore synchronization, but require more shared memory. Table 7.8 lists the resulting performance figures in frames per second for different Laplacian kernel sizes and software and hardware thread configurations. The *configuration* column indicates whether the threads (capture – laplace – display) have been run in software or hardware—the letters in parenthesis correspond to the configurations shown in Figure 7.3. For the SW-HW-HW* configurations, double-buffering has been enabled.

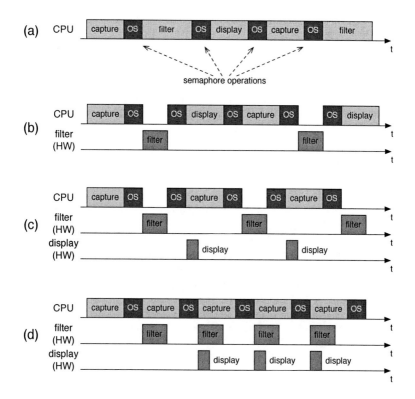

Figure 7.3: Thread-level parallelism for different configurations of the image processing case study. (a) All processing done is in software. (b) The filter thread is executed in hardware. (c) Both the filter and the display thread process in hardware. (d) Through double buffering, the filter and display threads can execute simultaneously.

We observe that by switching from a 3×3 to a 5×5 Laplacian kernel the software filter's performance drops dramatically while the hardware filter can exploit more fine-grained parallelism and delivers an almost constant performance. Also, we see that the resulting overall speedups of the sequential (SW-HW-SW) configuration (marked in bold) are quite close to the theoretically achievable speedups of 1.4 and 2.7 mentioned above. This points to an acceptable overhead of the ReconOS system calls.

The performance of the application could be further improved by additional low-level optimizations. However, the case study serves to demonstrate that by moving data-intensive threads to hardware while maintaining the underlying programming model—and thus making changes to the remaining parts of the system unnecessary—, appealing performance increases can be achieved.

7.3.2 Sorting

As a second application, we have implemented a multithreaded sorting algorithm with ReconOS and mapped it to different host operating systems and underlying hardware architectures to demonstrate the portability of applications based on the ReconOS programming model. The application sorts a list of 2^{18} unsorted 32-bit integers using a combination of bubble sort and merge sort; the basic concept is depicted in Figure 7.4. First, the data is divided into 128 chunks, which are sorted individually using bubble sort. The resulting lists are then merged. To map this application onto our system, we divided it into two threads, one for the bubble sort routine, which has a software and a hardware implementation, and one for the merge operation, which is always performed in software. The threads communicate using shared memory and use message boxes for simultaneous synchronization and passing of buffer addresses. The application has been run on all three prototype platforms. All systems use exactly the same application code for both software and hardware threads, and differ only in OS specific software application stubs.

Three tests have been performed: the first running the sort thread in software (SW); the second running the sort thread in hardware (HW); and the third running two sort threads concurrently, one in software, the other in hardware (SW+HW). The results of the measurements are shown in Figure 7.4. In this figure, two times are given for each test and architecture, the first (bold) value denotes the time spent sorting, while the second corresponds to the merge time.

The first and last test, which perform (at least part of) the sorting routine in software, reveal, unsurprisingly, that the MicroBlaze processor performs the sort operation vastly slower than the PowerPC. However, when executing the

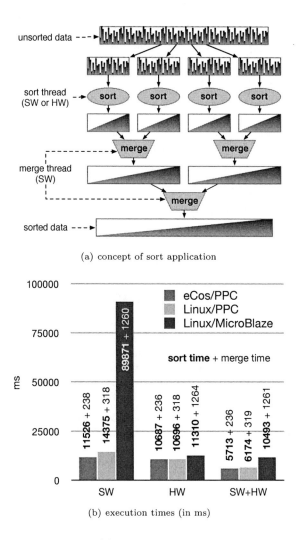

(a) concept of sort application

(b) execution times (in ms)

Figure 7.4: Sort case study. (a) Unsorted data is split into blocks which are sorted independently and then merged to form a sorted result. (b) Performance of the sort case study with three partitionings (SW, HW, SW+HW) on three different execution platforms (eCos/PPC, Linux/PPC, Linux/MicroBlaze).

sorting thread solely in hardware, all three systems are almost on par. In this situation, the hardware thread interacts with the OS synchronization primitives infrequently enough so that the performance penalty due to additional software processing remains within acceptable limits. This is a typical scenario: an application designer will likely use the precious hardware resources for data-centric computations with relatively infrequent OS synchronization operations, and perform most control-dominated tasks inside software threads. Therefore, while the penalty incurred by the low-level synchronization and communication between delegate thread and OS interface is substantial for OS calls alone, the effect on overall application performance is marginal.

This case study shows how the same multithreaded application description can be implemented on top of three different OS/processor platforms, effectively widening the choice of target platforms that can take advantage of the multi-threaded HW/SW programming model.

7.3.3 Sequential Monte-Carlo Framework

State estimation of non-linear dynamic systems is an important problem with applications in areas as diverse as object tracking, network packet processing, mobile communications and navigation systems. Of the available methods for solving this problem, sequential Monte Carlo (SMC) Methods—also called particle filters—enjoy widespread popularity and are frequently applied when a system's state is known only by its statistical distribution and can only be partially observed through possibly noisy measurements.

Despite their divergent application areas, all SMC methods follow the same fundamental algorithmic structure and thus share significant portions of common functionality. They track a number of possible state estimates, the *particles*, over time. These particles are continuously compared to measurements to determine the accuracy of the individual state estimates, and weighed accordingly. Usually, the quality of the state estimation can be improved by increasing the number of tracked particles.

In this section we present a framework for implementing particle filters on hybrid CPU/FPGA platforms which significantly simplifies the design of particle filters following the sampling importance resampling (SIR) algorithm. The framework handles the recurring tasks of particle data transfer and thread control, letting the designer focus on the application-specific details of an individual particle filter. Using the multithreaded programming model, the designer can quickly create different hardware/software partitionings to evaluate their performance and react to changing application and performance requirements.

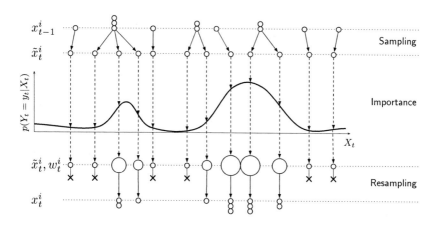

Figure 7.5: Sampling-Importance-Resampling algorithm [8].

SIR algorithm

Sequential Monte Carlo Methods estimate a system state x_t at time step t using probability distributions. We are considering that the system state is to be tracked in a dynamic environment and the initial distribution $p(X_0)$ is given, where X_0 is a random variable describing the state at time $t = 0$. The *system model* is a Markov process of first order. Thus, $p(X_t|X_{t-1})$ denotes the probability distribution of the system's current state given the system's previous state. We assume that the system state is hidden and can thus not be observed directly, but can be tracked by measurements y_t, which may be influenced by noise. The relation between measurements and system states is described by the *measurement model*. The distribution $p(Y_t = y_t|X_t)$ describes the probability of the current measurement given the system's current state. In other words, we make a statement about the likelihood of observing a specific measurement, provided we are in a system state modeled by X_t. The probability distribution of X_t is approximated by a fixed number of samples x_t^i, also called particles.

Figure 7.5 shows one iteration of the sampling importance resampling (SIR) algorithm for SMC methods, where particles are depicted as circles.

Sampling: The new particle state $\tilde{x}_t^i$ is drawn or *sampled* from the distribution

$$p(X_t|X_{t-1} = x_{t-1}^i).$$

Now, the set of particles $\tilde{x}_t^i$ forms a prediction of the distribution of X_t.

Importance: The measurement model is evaluated for every particle to determine the *likelihood* that the current measurement y_t matches the predicted state $\tilde{x}_t^i$ of the particle. The resulting likelihood is assigned as a weight w_t^i to the particle. In Figure 7.5, particles with higher weights are drawn as larger circles.

Resampling: Particles with comparatively high weights are duplicated and particles with low weights are eliminated. The distribution of the resulting particles x_t^i approximates the distribution of the weighted particles before resampling.

For a more thorough discussion of the theoretical foundations of SMC methods we refer to [39].

Framework Design

Figure 7.6 shows the basic structure of an SIR implementation using our framework. The particles cycle through four stages, the three SIR filter stages sampling, importance, and resampling, and an additional observation stage. Each of these stages can have an arbitrary number of software and hardware threads. Based on our experiments, we expect that in many applications, determining the importance weight of a given measurement requires particle-specific preprocessing of the measurements and involves significant computational complexity. Since this can be done independently for every particle, we have added an additional observation stage (again split into an arbitrary number of hardware and software threads), which handles all necessary measurement preprocessing. Our tests show that this technique significantly improves the performance of our case studies.

Communication and synchronization between the threads of different stages is managed using message box primitives of ReconOS. The execution times of threads within the stages may vary due to data-dependencies, memory latencies, CPU load and other factors. The total number of particles is thus split into chunks of user-defined size, which form the atomic entries stored in the message boxes. This enables the framework to balance the load between the threads of a stage and at the same time keeps the communication overhead small.

The particle filter framework provides parallelization for the sampling, observation, importance, and resampling stages. The number of hardware and software threads for each stage can be freely chosen, except that there must be at least one thread in each stage. Generally, the number of threads will depend on the availability of computing resources, i.e. CPU utilization factors and logic area.

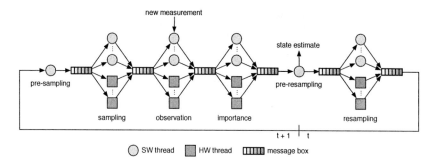

Figure 7.6: Iterative structure of the framework's SIR filter implementation. The sampling, observation, importance, and resampling stages are distributed among hardware and software threads. Single software threads (`preSampling` and `preResampling`) perform data reordering and state estimation.

The other threads of the framework are mainly control-dominated or show limited potential for parallelism and are therefore implemented in software. Access to the needed data, the control flow, as well as necessary operating system services for communication and synchronization are completely managed by the framework.

The relevant data structures and initial hardware partitioning is determined and initialized by a software thread, which also sets the initial number of threads for each stage.

Object Tracking

Tracking a moving object in a video sequence is a common task for state estimation methods. Using our framework, we have implemented a prototype system, using a software implementation by Hess [52] as a template and reference. Given an initial video frame, the user selects an object's initial position and its approximate outline in form of a bounding box. The particle filter then estimates the object's position and size in each subsequent frame of the video sequence. An example of the desired tracking behavior can be seen in Figure 7.7.

The state and measurement models and other application-specific parameters are defined as follows:

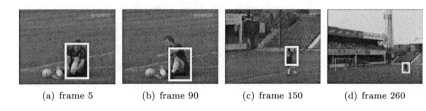

(a) frame 5   (b) frame 90   (c) frame 150   (d) frame 260

Figure 7.7: Example of object tracking in a video sequence. The highlighted particle indicates the best estimate of the soccer player's location and size.

Particle: A particle is composed of the horizontal and vertical coordinates x and y of the object's center pixel and the scaling factor s for the bounding box. The height and width of the original bounding box, as well as the first derivatives v_x, v_y, v_s are also stored in the particle to later compute $p(X_t|X_{t-1})$.

System model: The values for x, y, s, v_x, v_y and v_s are predicted as follows, where u_{α_t} models the system noise:

$$\left.\begin{aligned} \alpha_t &= \alpha_{t-1} + v_{\alpha_{t-1}} + u_{\alpha_t} \\ v_{\alpha_t} &= \alpha_t - \alpha_{t-1} \\ u_{\alpha_t} &\sim \mathcal{N}(0,\sigma^2) \end{aligned}\right\} \alpha \in \{x,y,s\}$$

Measurement: In each iteration, a user function reads a new frame from the video sequence.

Observation: The threads of the observation stage extract hue / saturation / value (HSV) color histogram data from the measured video frames, distinguishing between colored and uncolored pixels. The histogram data for particle i is stored in an array $H_i(k)$, $k = 0,\dots,l-1$.

Reference data: The reference data is the histogram $H_R(k)$ of the object selected by the user in the first frame.

Likelihood function: To calculate the *likelihood*, the histogram $H_i(k)$ of the estimated frame region is compared with the reference histogram $H_R(k)$ using the equation:

$$w_t^i = \exp^{-\left(1- \sum_{0 \leq k < l} \sqrt{(H_i(k)H_R(k))}\right)}$$

Thus, the likelihood value assigned to a particle depends exponentially on the similarity between the particle histogram and the histogram of the reference object.

The video data is stored on a PC, converted to HSV color space and transferred via Ethernet to the prototype boards. There, the data is cached in local SDRAM, processed, and output to a VGA controller or sent back to the PC via Ethernet. The output includes a bounding box framing the most likely estimate, which is derived from the average of all particles after each importance step.

The HW/SW partitioning of the individual filter stages has a direct impact on the attainable performance. The performance prediction for a specific partitioning or the identification of an optimal partitioning is a rather involved problem, and mostly the performance is even data-dependent. Thus, a designer will implement the required functions in software and/or hardware and then experiment with different HW/SW partitionings, which can be time-consuming. Here, our framework with its underlying multithreaded programming model assists the designer and allows him to quickly synthesize and evaluate different partitionings.

In this application, placing the sampling or resampling stages in hardware does not yield any performance improvements; for simplicity, these partitionings have not been included in the discussion. Instead, we have focused on the nine hardware/software partitionings shown in Table 7.9.

Partitioning	
sw	All threads run in software.
hw_i	One importance thread executes in hardware.
hw_{ii}	Two importance threads execute in hardware.
hw_o	One observation thread executes in hardware.
hw_{oo}	Two observation threads execute in hardware.
hw_{oi}	One observation thread, one importance thread in hw
hw_{ooi}	Two observation threads, one importance thread in hw
hw_{oii}	One observation threads, two importance threads in hw
hw_{ooii}	Two observation threads, two importance threads in hw

Table 7.9: HW/SW partitionings for the object tracking application.

Figure 7.8 shows the performance of the individual partitionings measured in clock cycles per frame. The measurements were performed on the soccer video sequence displayed in Figure 7.7.

During the first 100 frames of the sequence, the soccer player fills a large part of the video frame. Consequently, the bounding boxes maintained by

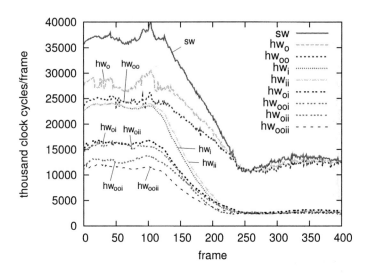

Figure 7.8: Object tracking run time of different static partitionings.

the particles are rather large, making the histogram computation expensive. Over the course of the next 150 frames, the soccer player retreats into the background, causing the scaling factor of the particles to diminish. Therefore, the histogram calculations are performed on smaller bounding boxes which explains the drop in necessary clock cycles per frame. Finally, as the player remains at about the same distance during the remainder of the video sequence, the number of clock cycles per frame levels out.

It can be seen that the performance gain obtained by placing one importance thread in hardware is data-independent across the entire video sequence. This is to be expected, as in this stage two fixed-sized histograms are compared, regardless of the scaling factor. Executing the observation stage in a single hardware thread increases the performance when large amounts of pixel data have to be processed into histograms for a given frame, i.e. when a particle's scaling factor is high. Thus, a performance gain can only be achieved for the first 250 frames before the soccer player retreats into the background.

Because a stage's computations are independent for different particles, we can exploit thread-level parallelism by mapping multiple threads in hardware, provided that the preceding stages can sustain the required data bandwidth. Thus, multiple importance threads only improve performance if the observation stage is also parallelized at the same level, as shown in the measurements of the partitionings hw_{ooi}, hw_{oi} and hw_{ooii}.; otherwise, no additional performance gain is achieved (hw_{ii}, hw_{oii}).

In summary, we see that a single importance thread in hardware does increase the performance of the object tracker in general while the benefit of using one or more observation threads is data-dependent. This fact can be used for efficient utilization of the reconfigurable area, as discussed in the next section.

Adaptive Partitioning

Depending on the system and measurement models of a given application, individual stages of the SIR algorithm may benefit from a hardware implementation to a varying degree. Our framework simplifies the exploration of different HW/SW partitionings, the performance of which are often not easily predictable, through the transparent multithreaded approach explained in Chapter 6. However, in many applications, the performance of individual stage threads is not only difficult to predict, but data-dependent. Thus, a partitioning that is optimal at one point during the video sequence may at a different point be inferior to another partitioning. In this case, changing the HW/SW partitioning during runtime would increase the overall performance of the application. Additionally, if the application has to satisfy certain performance constraints, such as a predefined iteration frequency of the SIR algorithm, we can change the HW/SW partitioning during runtime to fulfill these constraints while optimizing the application's area usage.

To evaluate adaptive reconfiguration within our framework, we have enabled it for the object tracking case study presented in Section 7.3.3 using the non-preemptive multitasking model introduced in Section 6.3.1. Here, the HW/SW partitioning is changed by terminating unneeded hardware threads or creating new hardware threads, using the standard multithreading API. The dynamic reconfiguration process itself is transparently managed by the hardware scheduler. By estimating the performance of the observation stage based on the scaling factor of the particles, the application can decide whether the observation thread should be executed in hardware or software to satisfy a previously set performance requirement, while at the same time using as little of the reconfigurable area as possible, thus yielding more processing resources to other executing threads or applications running at a lower hardware scheduling priority.

The performance of an *adaptive* partitioning of the object tracking application optimizing area usage can be seen in Figure 7.9. At the beginning of the video,

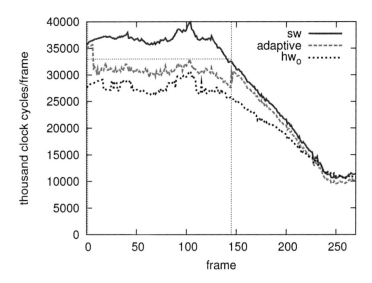

Figure 7.9: Object tracking run time of adaptive partitioning, compared to static *sw* and *hw*$_o$ partitionings. Reconfiguration occurs at frames 0 and 144; the horizontal line represents the performance requirement.

the comparably large scaling factor prompts the application to instantiate a hardware observation thread, similar to the *hw*$_o$ partitioning. This causes the frame processing time to drop below the performance requirement of 33×10^6 cycles per frame[3]. As soon as the soccer player retreats into the background, the scaling factor recedes below a threshold of 0.9. This allows the framework to switch back to a software-only partitioning, comparable to the *sw* partitioning, which performs good enough for the performance requirement but frees one slot in the reconfigurable logic to be used by other threads. Thus, by using adaptive reconfiguration of hardware threads, the application is able to make more efficient use of the system's resources.

---

[3]Because the additional bus macro logic required for partial reconfiguration adds additional latency to OS calls and memory accesses, the adaptive partitioning does not exactly reach the performance of the static *hw*$_o$ partitioning.

7.4 Chapter Conclusion

In summary, we have shown through several examples in this chapter that ReconOS is applicable to a wide range of application areas. We have used our prototype applications and case studies to demonstrate the prominent features of the ReconOS approach to multithreaded hardware/software co-design. Our incremental design approach allows the subsequent refinement of the hardware/software partitioning of an application, while the partial reconfiguration support can be used to apply these partitionings during run-time to exploit data-dependent performance characteristics. We have also shown that the ReconOS programming and execution environment remains portable across different CPU and operating system targets. Furthermore, we have quantified the area and timing overheads of the ReconOS interface components and mechanisms and argued that the overall impact on system performance remains acceptable due to the nature of typical hardware threads.

CHAPTER 8

Conclusions and Future Directions

In this chapter, we will summarize the contributions of this work, draw conclusions from the established results, and outline future research directions.

8.1 Contributions

Although the concept of operating system support for reconfigurable logic is not new, most approaches combining the two areas focused on the *management* of the reconfigurable area and mostly neglected the *integration* of hardware accelerators into the programming and execution environment. Also, research in run-time reconfigurability of FPGAs has been concentrated mainly on the topics of configuration management, technology improvements and low-level reconfiguration infrastructure, but comparably little progress has been made toward simplifying the programmability of fine-grained run-time reconfigurable architectures. Especially for modern FPGA-based systems that combine powerful microprocessors with reconfigurable fabrics, the discrepancies between the programming models for these heterogeneous environments have not been thoroughly addressed.

With this thesis, we present fundamental advancements in the area of programming reconfigurable CPU/FPGA platforms. In particular, we provide the following major contributions to the field:

- We have established the multithreaded programming paradigm—already popular and successful in the area of software operating systems—for the domain of reconfigurable hardware. We have presented a modeling

approach for hardware components, elevating them from passive coprocessors to autonomous hardware threads with full access to operating
system services for communication and synchronization. This modeling
approach also allows for effective integration of existing hardware accelerators into a multithreaded hardware/software system.

- We have designed and implemented a complete run-time environment
  that allows hardware threads to call blocking operating system functions
  in a transparent and intuitive manner without impairing their potential
  for fine-grained parallel execution. Our approach is the first to transparently support both fine-grained operation-level and more coarse-grained
  thread-level parallelism in a hybrid CPU/FPGA environment.

- We have integrated hardware thread support within two established embedded operating systems, eCos and Linux, taking into account specific
  differences such as virtual memory support, and thus leveraging a wide
  range of existing software applications and libraries.

- We have enabled the transparent use of modern FPGAs' partial reconfiguration features through the application of multithreaded programming.
  The decomposition of an application into hardware threads can be used
  for time-sharing the reconfigurable fabric of the target platform, either
  through explicit instantiation and termination of hardware threads under user control (non-preemptive multitasking), or through implicit replacement of inactive hardware threads with runnable ones (cooperative
  multitasking), controlled by the operating system.

- We provide an end-to-end tool flow integrating hardware and software
  thread descriptions with automated OS integration to generate both
  static and partially reconfigurable system architectures targeted at modern platform FPGAs. This tool flow also entails elaborate techniques for
  simulation, monitoring and debugging complex multithreaded hardware
  software systems.

By providing a unified programming model for both hardware and software
together with a complete end-to-end tool flow for generating both static and
partially reconfigurable multithreaded CPU/FPGA systems, we have taken a
step toward leveraging the potential of run-time reconfiguration and reduced
the productivity gap between the design flows for the hardware and software
parts of a modern reconfigurable system-on-chip. The tangible benefits of our
approach have been demonstrated through several experimental prototypes and
case studies and are actively employed in cooperating projects.

8.2 Conclusions

We draw the following conclusions from our work:

We have argued that, despite non-negligible overheads, our software-based approach to providing OS services to hardware enables the flexible creation and intuitive iterative refinement of hybrid applications. Our case studies show that the programming model primitives provided by established APIs are suitable for the seamless integration of hardware processing elements. These elements focus on data parallel processing tasks and therefore call OS functions for synchronization with a lower frequency than their software counterparts. Thus, the overheads in relaying OS calls to the software kernel, although substantial, do not significantly impede the capabilities of multithreaded hardware to improve overall system performance. We believe it necessary to provide designers without a hardware design background with a familiar paradigm for application decomposition and OS service interaction. Closing the gap between hardware and software development approaches can only improve the acceptance of reconfigurable platforms in the embedded systems domain.

At the same time, the multithreaded decomposition of a complex application into interacting threads provides a feasible modularization for partial reconfiguration. Current tool flows for partially reconfigurable systems require in-depth knowledge of FPGA design techniques and present a significant barrier of entry. With a suitably flexible run-time environment like ReconOS, much of the complexity of run-time reconfigurable systems can be encapsulated in the operating system and effectively hidden from the developer.

The methods of integrating hardware components within the synchronization schemes of a complex system have direct impact on the efficiency of the entire application. Existing scheduling techniques do not take the individual properties of such a heterogeneous and interdependent processing environment into account. We have shown that multitasking techniques—such as cooperative multithreading—that are inferior in conventional software-based systems may well prove to be a suitable alternative when applied to these novel execution environments.

8.3 Lessons Learned

During the development of and with ReconOS, we have gained the following personal experiences with multithreaded hardware/software development:

In both our own experience and that of our cooperation partners [4], the augmentation of hardware modules with a sequential FSM provided an easy-to-use method of integrating existing and new hardware accelerators into a multithreaded execution environment. The structured OS synchronization state machine with its explicit and encapsulated OS calls through VHDL procedures provided a very software-like and clear way to interact with the operating system. It appears that developers, even when accustomed to low-level hardware design in VHDL, appreciate the higher level of design abstraction when interacting with a otherwise software-based OS implementation. Furthermore, in conjunction with the established programming model primitives, the approach hides the underlying and often complex communication protocols required by the respective bus implementations, which otherwise often prove to be a major obstacle, especially for developers inexperienced in digital logic design.

During the development of prototypes and case studies, the flexible repartitioning of a system by moving threads between hardware and software without affecting the remaining system proved to be a valuable feature of ReconOS. The design approach allowed to quickly prototype a software-only system on a workstation, which then required relatively little effort to be moved onto the target FPGA board. In other words, this design-time adaptability allows us to apply a *"change is cheap"* design approach and thus a far more flexible, prototype-driven design flow than traditional approaches, where the hardware/software partitioning needs to be fixed well in advance.

A significant amount of development time was spent in following the changes introduced by the independently advancing versions of FPGA synthesis and implementation tools, experimental design flows, operating system kernels, and infrastructure utilities (e.g., parsers). The ReconOS environment represents a system of considerable complexity, and in several cases proved to be particularly sensitive to bugs or behavioral changes introduced in a seemingly unrelated section of the tool flow. Following established software engineering practices such as rigorous version control, automated regression testing and consistent feature encapsulation went a long way toward providing stability during changes of the ReconOS infrastructure or the underlying tool versions.

8.4 Future Directions

Based on the work presented in this thesis, we see several major directions of future research related to multithreaded programming of reconfigurable hardware:

Real-time systems: Many embedded systems are employed in a timing-critical context requiring real-time guarantees for execution times or function call latencies. Related work in real-time scheduling of reconfigurable hardware has been presented, for instance, by Danne [32]. By adapting the proposed thread models and scheduling techniques in conjunction with investigating the real-time properties of the ReconOS infrastructure, e.g., by following a hardware-based OS service approach similar to hthreads [86], opens an interesting research direction toward real-time capable multithreaded reconfigurable systems.

Self-adaptivity: The possibilites for a run-time reconfigurable system to adapt its hardware architecture to changing environmental conditions are manyfold. Complementary to changing the HW/SW partitioning of application threads, as we have demonstrated, conceivable approaches include the adaptation of the communication infrastructure or system layout, or the migration of entire parts of the OS' functionality into hardware. Also, the transparent migration of threads between hardware and software, as for example investigated by Götz [45] is a promising approach. All these techniques require highly customizable monitoring and run-time profiling mechanisms as well as efficient prediction algorithms for deciding on the appropriate adaptation. So far, this area of research is mainly covered by simulation techniques, but lacks actual implementations of adaptive applications. We believe that ReconOS provides a suitable customizable platform for exploring different venues of run-time adaptation.

Multi-CPU systems: Instead of combining a single CPU with multiple execution slots for hardware threads, the reconfigurable fabric could also be used for instantiating multiple CPUs. This approach is, for example, followed by current developments in the hthreads project [14], and has also already been investigated in conjunction with ReconOS [74], providing a truly parallel execution environment for both hardware and software threads. Interesting research questions in this area include the partitioning of OS services across multiple CPUs, combined hardware/software scheduling approaches, and the run-time reconfiguration and FPGA resource sharing of soft-core CPUs and hardware threads.

Domain-specific abstractions: While the integration of hardware threads into the operating system has been bound to a familiar programming model, the actual development of ReconOS hardware threads is still a hardware design process, albeit augmented with software-derived constructs. As the availability of domain-specific synthesis tools [105, 119] increases, their integration into the multithreaded hardware design process appears to be a promising research direction. Some domain-specific approaches are already capable of generating multithreaded code [47], which could be further developed into synthesizing multithreaded hardware.

High-performance computing: Although this thesis focuses on systems in the embedded domain, its principles are just as applicable to high-performance computing (HPC). In the HPC domain, designers already deal with highly parallel algorithms, often implemented in distributed processing environments. In a computing cluster containing nodes augmented with reconfigurable hardware, the application of multithreading as a unified programming model is an interesting topic and bears novel research questions regarding communication and synchronization techniques on high-performance architectures.

In general, we believe that the ReconOS programming model and execution platform represent a flexible, extensible, and comparably easy-to-use environment for further research related to hybrid reconfigurable systems and run-time reconfigurability. While multithreading is not the only choice for programming parallel systems, it has gained widespread acceptance both as a direct development model as well as a common foundation for implementing other languages [49, 50, 98]. Its extension to reconfigurable logic advertises FPGAs as another promising implementation target for both established and new techniques for designing parallel applications.

Tools and File Formats

The appendix contains additional detailed information regarding the platform and simulation descriptions as well as the tools used by ReconOS. The following sections detail:

- the **command definition** (CMDDEF) syntax specifying the delegate thread code fragments for OS specific implementations of hardware-initiated operating system calls (see Section 5.2.2)

- the **slot stimulus** (SST) syntax used by the hardware thread simulation model (see Section 5.3)

- the **layout file** (LYT) syntax employed for the automatic generation of implementation constraints required by the partial reconfiguration tool flow (see Section 6.6.1)

- the **project** (PRJ) file syntax for globally controlling the automated tool flow and specifying project-wide parameters

Furthermore, table A.2 on page 166 lists the most important tools used by the ReconOS tool chain and their purpose.

A.1 Command Definitions

A command definition file combines all necessary information about software-handled operating system calls available to hardware threads in a central location. Listing A.1 shows the command definition of the `reconos_mbox_put()`

159

operation as an example. After defining general properties of the command, it provides the necessary information for automatic generation of the associated delegate thread code, such as needed header files. In particular, a command definition includes:

- the command's *verbose* (line 5) and *symbolic* (line 7) names,

- its hexadecimal *encoding* (line 8),

- a *type* field and *options* (lines 9f.), such as whether the command is blocking (`BLOCKING`) or has a return value (`RETVAL`), and

- several *delegate* blocks (`DELEGATE`, lines 12ff., 21ff., 55ff.) containing the software implementation details for different operating systems, such as:

  − the target *host operating system* (`HOST_OS`, e.g., eCos or Linux),

  − the associated *resource type* (`RESTYPE`),

  − all necessary *header files* (`HEADER`),

  − encapsulating *preprocessor directives* (`IFDEF`) for integration into the configuration framework, and

  − *code* implementing the command's functionality with the respective operating system's API (`CODE`).

The code itself contains placeholders (starting with '$') for the data fields received from the OSIF, the resources array, and a possible return value. Identical code for different host OS implementations, such as for eCos using the POSIX API and Linux, can be shared using the COPY_CODE directive (line 59).

Command definitions are used for automatic generation of the delegate thread's code, as detailed in Section 5.2.2.

```
 1  #
 2  # mbox_put.cmddef:  command definition for mbox put operations
 3  #
 4
 5  COMMAND reconos_mbox_put
 6
 7       SYMBOL          OSIF_CMD_MBOX_PUT
 8       ENCODING        0x87
 9       TYPE            TASK2OS
10       OPTIONS         BLOCKING RETVAL
11
12       DELEGATE ecos_ecos
13            HOST_OS              ecos
14            RESTYPE              CYG_MBOX_HANDLE_T
15            HEADER               <cyg/kernel/kapi.h>
```

```
16          HEADER                  <cyg/infra/cyg_type.h>
17          CODE                    "$retval = (uint32)cyg_mbox_put(*(( \
18          cyg_handle_t*)$resources[$data].ptr), (void *)$datax);"
19  END # ecos_ecos
20
21  DELEGATE ecos_posix
22          HOST_OS                 ecos
23          RESTYPE                 PTHREAD_MQD_T
24          HEADER                  <cyg/posix/types.h>
25          HEADER                  <fcntl.h>
26          HEADER                  <mqueue.h>
27          IFDEF                   UPBFUN_RECONOS_POSIX
28          CODE '''
29              mqd_t q;
30              char * mqname;
31              struct mq_attr oldattr, newattr;
32
33              mqname = $resources[$data].ptr;
34              q = mq_open(mqname, O_WRONLY);
35              if(q == (mqd_t)(-1)){
36                      CYG_FAIL("error opening posix mq for writing");
37                      break;
38              }
39
40              // set queue to be blocking
41              mq_getattr(q, &oldattr);
42              newattr = oldattr;
43              newattr.mq_flags = newattr.mq_flags & ~O_NONBLOCK;
44              mq_setattr(q, &newattr, NULL);
45              if (mq_send(q, (char*) &$datax, 4, 0) < 0) {
46                      $retval = 0;     // signal error
47              } else {
48                      $retval = 1;     // signal success
49              }
50              // restore old queue attributes
51              mq_setattr(q, &oldattr, NULL);
52          '''
53  END # ecos_posix
54
55  DELEGATE linux_posix
56          HOST_OS                 linux
57          RESTYPE                 PTHREAD_MQD_T
58          HEADER                  <mqueue.h>
59          COPY_CODE               ecos_posix
60  END #linux_posix
61
62  END # reconos_mbox_put
```

Listing A.1: Example of a command definition.

Command	Description
OS-to-thread	
`write_init_data`	Set the initialization word of the thread
`write_unlock` [*retval*]	Unblock a waiting thread, with optional return value
`write_resume` *state step*	Resume a yielding thread at a certain *state* and *step*
`request_yield`	Request the thread to yield, if possible
`clear_yield`	Cancel a pending yield request
`write_fifo_{read/write}_handle`	Set resource indices for incoming/outgoing FIFOs
`write_busmacro` *value*	Enable or disables the thread's bus macros
`reset`	Reset the thread and the OSIF state
`wait` *timespec*	Wait for *timespec* until executing the next command
Thread-to-OS	
`read_thread_yield`	Expect a thread yield request
`read_thread_delay` *ticks*	Expect a thread delay request
`read_sem_wait` *sem_id*	Expect a semaphore wait request
`read_shm_post` *shm_id*	Expect a semaphore post request
`read_mutex_lock` *mutex_id*	Expect a mutex lock request
`read_mutex_unlock` *mutex_id*	Expect a mutex unlock request
`read_mutex_trylock` *mutex_id*	Expect a mutex trylock request
`read_mutex_release` *mutex_id*	Expect a mutex release request
`read_cond_wait` *condvar_id*	Expect a condition variable wait request
`read_cond_signal` *condvar_id*	Expect a condition variable signal request
`read_cond_broadcast` *condvar_id*	Expect a condition variable broadcast request
`read_mbox_get` *mbox_id*	Expect a mailbox get request
`read_mbox_tryget` *mbox_id*	Expect a mailbox tryget request
`read_mbox_put` *mbox_id*	Expect a mailbox put request
`read_mbox_tryput` *mbox_id*	Expect a mailbox tryput request
`read_mq_receive` *mbox_id offset size*	Expect a message queue receive request
`read_mq_send` *mbox_id offset size*	Expect a message queue send request

Table A.1: Slot stimulus commands.

A.2 Slot Stimuli

In a slot stimulus file, the thread developer statically specifies the sequence of software-handled system calls the hardware thread is *expected* to perform during the simulation and the appropriate responses from the operating system. The purpose of this file is to stimulate the bus inputs of the OSIF to imitate OS behavior, and to automatically verify the thread's interactions with the OS. In this way, a complete simulation of the entire software operating system (and the CPU) can be avoided, significantly shortening simulation time.

A slot stimulus file consists of a list of commands sequentially performed by either the operating system (`write_*`) or the hardware thread (`read_*`). The commands can be separated by `wait` commands to simulate OS or thread activity during or between OS calls, respectively. When expecting thread activity, the respective thread OS call request must have occurred before reaching the `read_*` command, and its parameters must match the SST command's parameters exactly. An example of a slot stimulus file can be found in Listing 5.1 on page 93. Table A.1 lists the available SST commands, grouped by initiator (OS or thread). Memory requests do not appear in this list, as they are handled independently from the OS kernel in hardware by the OSIF.

The SST files are parsed by the `mkbfmtb` and `mkbfl` tools during simulation setup.

A.3 Layout File

Due to the physical topology of the configuration infrastructure of Xilinx FP-GAs, the early-access partial reconfiguration (EAPR) tool chain provided by Xilinx relies on the designer to comply with detailed constraints regarding the placement of reconfigurable areas, interface logic, and clock trees. Within these constraints, the size, shape, and location of the reconfigurable areas, which will subsequently contain the individual hardware threads' logic, can be freely chosen to match the requirements of the application. To simplify the manual adaptation of user constraints files (UCFs) used by the Xilinx tools, the ReconOS tool chain provides a layout file format to specify the area parameters for reconfigurable regions.

A layout file encapsulates all necessary information about the physical placement of reconfigurable regions by specifying the target device and the area constraints for one or more slots. Listing A.2 outlines the syntax of a layout file with an example. It contains a `TARGET` block, specifying the device (e.g., XC2VP30) and the device family (e.g., XC2VP for Virtex-II-Pro) to select the appropriate bus macro libraries. Following the target block, one or more `SLOT` blocks specify the individual reconfigurable regions, or slots, of the architecture to be generated.

```
1   # Reconos FPGA layout file (version 3.1.0a)
2
3   TARGET
4           DEVICE XC2VP30
5           FAMILY xc2vp
6   END
7
8   SLOT HW_TASK_0
9           SLICE_RANGE SLICE_X12Y112:SLICE_X33Y145
```

```
10              RANGE MULT18x18 MULT18x18_X1Y14:MULT18x18_X2Y17
11              RANGE RAMB16 RAMB16_X1Y14:RAMB16_X2Y17
12
13      # input
14              BUSMACRO
15                      TYPE r2l_sync_wide
16                      LOC X30Y112
17              END
18
19      # ... input bus macros ...
20
21      # output
22              BUSMACRO
23                      TYPE l2r_sync_enable_narrow
24                      LOC X32Y112
25              END
26
27      # ... output bus macros ...
28
29      END
30
31      SLOT hw_task_1
32              SLICE_RANGE SLICE_X60Y112:SLICE_X81Y145
33              RANGE MULT18x18 MULT18x18_X5Y14:MULT18x18_X6Y17
34              RANGE RAMB16 RAMB16_X5Y14:RAMB16_X6Y17
35
36      # ... bus macros ...
37
38      END
```

Listing A.2: Example layout file.

In a `SLOT` description, individual `RANGE` clauses specify the placement constraints for special blocks, such as `DSP48`, `RAMB16`, `FIFO16`, or `MULT18x18`, depending on the presence of the corresponding resources within the reconfigurable region. The actual ranges follow the syntax of regular area constraints as used in a Xilinx UCF description.

Also, the type and placement of the required interface bus macros are specified within a `SLOT` block. There are several types of bus macros, owing to the possible combinations of the following features:

Direction: Depending on the location on the boundary of the reconfigurable region, bus macros can be oriented left-to-right (`l2r`) or right-to-left (`r2l`).

Register: To ease timing closure for control signals, bus macros can include registers within the signal path (`sync`) or omit them (`async`).

Enable: Signals initiating within a hardware thread and interfacing with logic in the OSIF induce a risk of inadvertently toggling during reconfiguration. This can be avoided using bus macros with explicit enable input (`enable`).

Span: Narrow (`narrow`) bus macros span exactly two adjacent CLBs, while wide (`wide`) bus macros span three CLBs, allowing for horizontal nesting of bus macros for reconfigurable regions of limited height.

Examples of bus macro types are:

`r2l_sync_enable_wide`: An output bus macro with a register in the signal path, located on the left side of the reconfigurable region.

`r2l_sync_wide`: An input bus macro—hence no enable—on the right side of the reconfigurable region, including registers in the signal path.

`l2r_async_enable_narrow`: A typical narrow output bus macro situated on the right edge of a reconfigurable region for connecting RAM signals of the hardware thread which need to be asynchronous to achieve high throughput.

The number of bus macros is determined by the amount of interface signals between OSIF and hardware thread. Each bus macro can connect up to 8 signals of a given type, adding up to a required number of 17 incoming and 15 outgoing bus macros (see also Section 7.2.1). Any incompatibilities between the layout file and the ReconOS requirements are verbosely reported by the tool chain.

The layout file is later used by the ReconOS tool chain to generate the user constraints files (UCFs) and insert the necessary interface logic into the top level design, as required by the EAPR flow (refer to Section 6.6.1 for details).

A.4 Project File

A project file, as exemplarily shown in Listing A.3, defines project-wide parameters for the ReconOS tool chain, such as the reference design to be used as a basis, the static and dynamic hardware threads to integrate, as well as command line parameters for the individual tools.

The project defined by the given example is targeted at a Xilinx ML403 board and uses a reference design prepared for partial reconfiguration (hence the `_pr` suffix, line 2). The shown file also determines the system's layout (line 3, see Appendix A.3), hardware thread location (line 4), and various tool parameters such as the effort to be put into the map, place, and route phases of the Xilinx implementation flow (lines 9 and 10) or the global clock signals for the system's hardware threads (lines 11 and 12). Also, the names of the hardware thread descriptions to be integrated either as statically mapped threads (line 6) or as dynamically reconfigurable threads (line 7) can be found in this file.

```
1  # ReconOS project file (format v1.00.a)
2  EDK_BASE_DIR = $(RECONOS)/hw/refdesigns/9.2/ml403/ml403_light_pr
3  LAYOUT = pr_demo_xc4vfx12.lyt
4  HW_THREAD_DIR = hwthreads
5
6  STATIC_THREADS=thread_a thread_b
7  DYNAMIC_THREADS=thread_c thread_d thread_e
8
9  PAROPTS = -ol high -w
10 MAPOPTS = -ol high -timing
11 ADDTHREAD_OPTS = -o sys_clk_s
12 MAKETOP_OPTS = --no-slot-bufg
```

Listing A.3: Example project file.

Starting from the reference design (line 2), the ReconOS tool chain thus automatically assembles, synthesizes, places, and routes the described system together with all necessary infrastructure components such as OSIFs, bus macros, and clock buffers to form a static and/or partially reconfigurable system.

Tool	Description
Platform generation	
maketop	Insert PR infrastructure into top-level VHDL description
makeucf	Insert PR area constraints from layout file into UCF
mhsaddfifo	Insert FIFO into EDK platform description
mhsaddosif	Insert OSIF into EDK platform description
mhsaddthread	Insert hardware thread into EDK platform description
mssaddriver	Insert software driver into EDK platform description
mkhwthread	Create IP core wrapper for hardware thread description
Simulation	
mkbfl	Create bus functional language file from slot stimulus
mkbfmsim	Create BFM simulation infrastructure for hardware thread
mkbfmtb	Create or modify VHDL test bench (simulated CPU) from slot stimulus
Miscellaneous	
bit2c	Turn bit file into static linkable C array
mkprj	Create ReconOS project directory structure

Table A.2: ReconOS tools.

Acronyms

AES	advanced encryption standard
AMBA	advanced microcontroller bus architecture
API	application programmer interface
ASIC	application-specific integrated circuit
ASIP	application-specific instruction-set processor
BFL	bus functional language
BFM	bus functional model
BRAM	block RAM
BSP	board support package
BUFG	global clock buffer
CAM	content-addressable memory
CDL	configuration description language
CLB	configurable logic block
CMDDEF	command definition [file]
CPLD	complex programmable logic device
CPU	central processing unit
DCM	digital clock manager
DCR	device control register [bus]
DMA	direct memory access
DPR	dynamic partial reconfiguration
DSP	digital signal processor
DSR	deferred service routine
EAPR	early-access partial reconfiguration [tool flow]
EDF	earliest-deadline-first
EDK	embedded development kit
(E)EPROM	(electrically) erasable programmable ROM
ESM	Erlangen Slot Machine
FF	flip-flop
FIFO	first-in first-out [storage element]
FPGA	field-programmable gate array
FSM	finite state machine
GCC	GNU C compiler
HDL	hardware description language
HLL	high-level language
HLS	high-level synthesis
HPC	high-performance computing

HSV	hue / saturation / value [color space]
HW	hardware
HWT-MMU	hardware thread MMU
ICAP	internal configuration access port
IOB	input/output block
IP	intellectual property
IPC	inter-process communication
ISR	interrupt service routine
JTAG	Joint Test Action Group [debug interface]
LUT	look-up table
LYT	layout [file]
MAC	multiply-accumulate [operation]
MMU	memory management unit
MPGA	mask-programmable gate array
MSI	medium-scale integration
MUX	multiplexer
OPB	on-chip peripheral bus
OS	operating system
OSIF	operating system interface
PAL	programmable array logic
PLB	processor local bus
PLD	programmable logic device
PP	peripheral processor
PPC	PowerPC [processor]
PR	partial reconfiguration
PRJ	project [file]
PTE	page table entry
PTW	page table walk
RAM	random-access memory
ROM	read-only memory
RTL	register-transfer level
SDRAM	synchronous dynamic RAM
SIR	sampling importance resampling [algorithm]
SMC	sequential Monte Carlo [method]
SMT	simultaneous multithreading
SoC	system-on-chip
SoPC	system-on-programmable chip
SPLD	simple programmable logic device
SRAM	static RAM
SRMP	shared memory multiprocessor
SSI	small-scale integration
SST	slot stimulus [file]
SW	software
TCP/IP	transmission control protocol / internet protocol
TLB	translation look-aside buffer
UCF	user constraints [file]
VHDL	VHSIC hardware description language
VHSIC	very high speed integrated circuit

Bibliography

Author's Publications

[1] Enno Lübbers. FlexFilm-DDR-SDRAM-Controller: Anbindung an den PowerPC 405 im Virtex-II Pro. Diploma thesis, Technische Universität Braunschweig, Oct 2005.

[2] Enno Lübbers and Marco Platzner. ReconOS: An RTOS Supporting Hard- and Software Threads. In *IEEE International Conference on Field Programmable Logic and Applications (FPL'07)*. IEEE, Aug 2007.

[3] Tobias Schumacher, Enno Lübbers, Paul Kaufmann, and Marco Platzner. Accelerating the Cube Cut Problem with an FPGA-augmented Compute Cluster. In *International Conference on Parallel Computing (ParCo'07), ParaFPGA Symposium*, Oct 2007.

[4] J. Angermeier, M. Majer, J. Teich, L. Braun, T. Schwalb, P. Graf, M. Hübner, J. Becker, E. Lübbers, M. Platzner, C. Claus, W. Stechele, A. Herkersdorf, M. Rullmann, and R. Merker. SPP1148 Booth: Fine Grain Reconfigurable Architectures. In *IEEE International Conference on Field Programmable Logic and Applications (FPL'08)*, page 348. IEEE, Aug 2008.

[5] Enno Lübbers and Marco Platzner. A Portable Abstraction Layer for Hardware Threads. In *IEEE International Conference on Field Programmable Logic and Applications (FPL'08)*, pages 17–22. IEEE, Aug 2008.

[6] Enno Lübbers and Marco Platzner. Communication and Synchronization in Multithreaded Reconfigurable Computing Systems. In *8th International Conference on Engineering of Reconfigurable Systems and Algorithms (ERSA'08)*, pages 1–7. CSREA Press, May 2008.

[7] Tobias Schumacher, Robert Meiche, Paul Kaufmann, Enno Lübbers, Christian Plessl, and Marco Platzner. A Hardware Accelerator for k-th Nearest Neighbor Thinning. In *8th International Conference on Engineering of Reconfigurable Systems and Algorithms (ERSA'08)*. CSREA Press, 2008.

[8] Markus Happe, Enno Lübbers, and Marco Platzner. A Multithreaded Framework for Sequential Monte Carlo Methods on CPU/FPGA Platforms. In *5th International Workshop on Reconfigurable Computing: Architectures, Tools and Applications (ARC'09)*, pages 380–385, 2009.

[9] Markus Happe, Enno Lübbers, and Marco Platzner. An Adaptive Sequential Monte Carlo Framework with Runtime HW/SW Repartitioning. In *IEEE International Conference on Field Programmable Technology (FPT'09)*. IEEE, Dec 2009.

[10] Enno Lübbers and Marco Platzner. Cooperative Multithreading in Dynamically Reconfigurable Systems. In *IEEE International Conference on Field Programmable Logic and Applications (FPL'09)*, pages 1–4. IEEE, 2009.

[11] Enno Lübbers and Marco Platzner. ReconOS: Multithreaded Programming for Reconfigurable Computers. *ACM Transactions on Embedded Computing Systems (TECS)*, 9(1), October 2009.

[12] Enno Lübbers and Marco Platzner. ReconOS: An Operating System for Dynamically Reconfigurable Hardware. *Dynamically Reconfigurable Systems: Architectures, Design Methods and Applications*, Springer, 2010. ISBN: 978-90-481-3484-7.

Bibliography

[13] Andreas Agne. Virtuelle Speicherverwaltung für Hardware Threads in Rekonfigurierbaren Systemen. Diploma thesis, Universität Paderborn, 2009.

[14] Jason Agron. Building Heterogeneous Reconfigurable Systems Using Threads. In *IEEE International Conference on Field Programmable Logic and Applications (FPL)*. IEEE, 2009.

[15] Jason Agron and David Andrews. Building Heterogeneous Reconfigurable Systems with a Hardware Microkernel. In *7th IEEE/ACM International Conference on Hardware/Software Codesign and System Synthesis (CODES+ISSS)*. IEEE, Oct 2009.

[16] Jason Agron, Wesley Peck, Erik Anderson, David Andrews, Ed Komp, Ron Sass, Fabrice Baijot, and Jim Stevens. Run-Time Services for Hybrid CPU/FPGA Systems on Chip. In *27th International Real-Time Systems Symposium (RTSS)*, pages 3–12. IEEE, 2006.

[17] Erik Anderson, Wesley Peck, Jim Stevens, Jason Agron, Fabrice Baijot, Seth Warn, and David Andrews. Supporting High Level Language Semantics within Hardware Resident Threads. In *17th IEEE International Conference on Field Programmable Logic and Applications (FPL)*, volume 1, pages 98–103. IEEE, Aug 2007.

[18] K. Bazargan, R. Kastner, and M. Sarrafzadeh. Fast Template Placement for Reconfigurable Computing Systems. *IEEE Design & Test of Computers*, 17(1):68–83, 2000.

[19] Neil W. Bergmann, John A. Williams, Jie Han, and Yi Chen. A Process Model for Hardware Modules in Reconfigurable System-on-Chip. In *19th International Conference on Architecture of Computing Systems, Dynamically Reconfigurable Systems Workshop*, volume 81, pages 205–214, Mar 2006.

[20] V. Berman. The P1685 IP-XACT IP Metadata Standard. *IEEE Design & Test of Computers*, 23:316–317, 2006.

[21] M. Boden, T. Fiebig, T. Meissner, and S. Rülke. High-Level Synthesis of HW Tasks Targeting Run-Time Reconfigurable FPGAs. In *International Parallel and Distributed Processing Symposium (IPDPS)*. IEEE, Jan 2007.

[22] C. Bolchini, A. Miele, and M. Santambrogio. TMR and Partial Dynamic Reconfiguration to Mitigate SEU Faults in FPGAs. In *IEEE International Symposium on Defect and Fault-Tolerance in VLSI Systems (DFT)*. IEEE, Jan 2007.

[23] Gordon Brebner. The Swappable Logic Unit: A Paradigm for Virtual Hardware. In *IEEE Symposium on FPGAs for Custom Computing Machines (FCCM)*, pages 77–86. IEEE, 1997.

[24] Gordon J. Brebner. A Virtual Hardware Operating System for the Xilinx XC6200. In *6th International Workshop on Field-Programmable Logic and Applications (FPL)*, pages 327–336, London, UK, 1996. Springer-Verlag.

[25] Stephen D. Brown, Robert J. Francis, Jonathan Rose, and Zvonko G. Vranesic. *Field-Programmable Gate Arrays*. Kluwer Academic Publishers, 1992.

[26] Jim Burns, Adam Donlin, Jonathan Hogg, Satnam Singh, and Mark de Wit. A Dynamic Reconfiguration Run-Time System. In *IEEE Symposium on FPGAs for Custom Computing Machines (FCCM)*, pages 66–75. IEEE, 1997.

[27] Celoxica. Handel-C. Website, 2006. `http://www.celoxica.com`.

[28] C. Claus, F.H. Muller, J. Zeppenfeld, and W. Stechele. A New Framework to Accelerate Virtex-II Pro Dynamic Partial Self-Reconfiguration. In *IEEE International Parallel and Distributed Processing Symposium (IPDPS)*, pages 1–7. IEEE, 2007.

[29] Katherine Compton, Zhiyuan Li, James Cooley, Stephen Knol, and Scott Hauck. Configuration Relocation and Defragmentation for Run-Time Reconfigurable Computing. *IEEE Transactions on Very Large Scale Integration (VLSI) Systems*, 10(3):209–220, Jun 2002.

[30] Harris Corporation. Falcon II VHF Handheld Digital Radio. Website, 2010. `http://www.rfcomm.harris.com/news/view_pressrelease.asp?act=lookup&pr_id=923`.

[31] Intel Corporation. Intel HyperThreading Technology. Website, 2010. `http://www.intel.com/technology/platform-technology/hyper-threading/`.

[32] Klaus Danne. *Real-Time Multitasking in Embedded Systems Based on Reconfigurable Hardware*. PhD thesis, University of Paderborn, 2006.

[33] Klaus Danne, Roland Mühlenbernd, and Marco Platzner. Server-based Execution of Periodic Tasks on Dynamically Reconfigurable Hardware. *IET Computers & Digital Techniques*, 1(4):295–302, Jul 2007.

[34] Klaus Danne and Marco Platzner. A Heuristic Approach to Schedule Periodic Real-time Tasks on Reconfigurable Hardware. In *15th IEEE International Conference on Field Programmable Logic and Applications (FPL)*. IEEE, 2005.

[35] Klaus Danne and Marco Platzner. An EDF Schedulability Test for Periodic Tasks on Reconfigurable Hardware Devices. In *ACM SIGPLAN/SIGBED Conference on Languages, Compilers, and Tools for Embedded Systems (LCTES)*, Ottawa, Canada, Jun 2006. ACM.

[36] André DeHon. Balancing Interconnect and Computation in a Reconfigurable Computing Array (or, Why You Don't Really Want 100% LUT Utilization). In *1999 ACM/SIGDA Seventh International Symposium on*

Field Programmable Gate Arrays (FPGA), pages 69–78, New York, NY, USA, 1999. ACM.

[37] O. Diessel, H. ElGindy, M. Middendorf, H. Schmeck, and B. Schmidt. Dynamic Scheduling of Tasks on Partially Reconfigurable FPGAs. *IEE Proceedings – Computers and Digital Techniques*, 147(3):181–188, May 2000.

[38] Amilcar do Carmo Lucas, Sven Heithecker, Peter Rüffer, Rolf Ernst, Holger Rückert, Gerhard Wischermann, Karin Gebel, Reinhard Fach, Wolfgang Huther, Stefan Eichner, and Gunter Scheller. A Reconfigurable HW/SW Platform for Computation Intensive High-Resolution Real-Time Digital Film Applications. In *IEEE International Conference on Design Automation and Test in Europe (DATE)*, pages 194–199. IEEE, 2006.

[39] Arnaud Doucet, Nando de Freitas, and Neil Gordon. *Sequential Monte Carlo Methods in Practice*. Springer, 2001.

[40] eCosCentric. eCos. Website, 2008. http://ecos.sourceware.org/.

[41] Stephen A. Edwards. The Challenges of Synthesizing Hardware from C-Like Languages. *IEEE Design & Test of Computers*, 23(5):375–386, 2006.

[42] E. El-Araby, I. Gonzalez, and T. El-Ghazawi. Virtualizing and Sharing Reconfigurable Resources in High-Performance Reconfigurable Computing Systems. In *Second International Workshop on High-Performance Reconfigurable Computing Technology and Applications (HPRCTA)*, pages 1–8, Nov 2008.

[43] S. Fekete, E. Köhler, and J. Teich. Optimal FPGA Module Placement With Temporal Precedence Constraints. In *IEEE International Conference on Design, Automation and Test in Europe (DATE)*, pages 658–667, Piscataway, NJ, USA, 2001. IEEE.

[44] Michael J. Flynn. *Computer Architecture: Pipelined and Parallel Processor Design*, chapter 8.7, pages 533–538. Jones and Bartlett Publishers, 1995.

[45] Marcelo Götz. *Run-time Reconfigurable RTOS for Reconfigurable Systems-on-Chip*. PhD thesis, University of Paderborn, 2007.

[46] S. Gupta, N. Dutt, R. Gupta, and A. Nicolau. SPARK: A High-Level Synthesis Framework for Applying Parallelizing Compiler Transformations. In *International Conference on VLSI Design (VLSI)*, Jan 2003.

[47] Sang-Il Han, Soo-Ik Chae, Lisane Brisolara, Luigi Carro, Ricardo Reis, Xavier Guérin, and Ahmed Amine Jerraya. Memory-Efficient Multi-threaded Code Generation from Simulink for Heterogeneous MPSoC. *Design Automation for Embedded Systems*, 11(4):249–283, 2007.

[48] Markus Happe. Parallelisierung und Hardware-/Software-Codesign von Partikelfiltern. Master's thesis, Universität Paderborn, 2008.

[49] Tim Harris, Simon Marlow, and Simon Peyton Jones. Haskell on a Shared-Memory Multiprocessor. In *2005 ACM SIGPLAN workshop on Haskell (Haskell)*, pages 49–61, New York, NY, USA, 2005. ACM.

[50] Pekka Hedqvist. A Parallel and Multithreaded ERLANG Implementation. Master's thesis, Uppsala University, 1998.

[51] John L. Hennessy and David A. Patterson. *Computer Architecture: A Quantitative Approach, Third Edition*, chapter 6.9, pages 608–615. Morgan Kaufmann Publishers, 2003.

[52] Rob Hess. Particle Filter Object Tracking, 2006. `http://web.engr.oregonstate.edu/~hess`.

[53] F. Iacomacci, C. Morlet, F. Autelitano, G. Cardarilli, M. Re, E. Petrongari, G. Bogo, and M. Franceschelli. A Software Defined Radio Architecture for a Regenerative On-Board Processor. In *NASA/ESA Conference on Adaptive Hardware and Systems (AHS)*, pages 164–171, 2008.

[54] IBM. CoreConnect Bus Architecture. Website, 2010. `https://www-01.ibm.com/chips/techlib/techlib.nsf/products/CoreConnect_Bus_Architecture`.

[55] IEEE and The Open Group. The Open Group Base Specifications Issue 6, IEEE Std. 1003.1, 2004 Edition, 2004.

[56] Inc. Impulse Accelerated Technologies. ImpulseC. Website, 2009. `http://www.impulsec.com`.

[57] J. S. N. Jean, K. Tomko, V. Yavagal, J. Shah, and R. Cook. Dynamic Reconfiguration to Support Concurrent Applications. *IEEE Transactions on Computers*, 48(6):591–602, 1999.

[58] S. Jovanovic, C. Tanougast, and S. Weber. A Hardware Preemptive Multitasking Mechanism Based on Scan-path Register Structure for FPGA-based Reconfigurable Systems. In *2nd NASA/ESA Conference on Adaptive Hardware and Systems (AHS)*, pages 358–364, 2007.

[59] Heiko Kalte and Mario Porrmann. Context Saving and Restoring for Multitasking in Reconfigurable Systems. In *IEEE International Conference on Field Programmable Logic and Applications (FPL)*, pages 223–228. IEEE, 2005.

[60] F. Kasperski, O. Pierrelee, F. Dotto, and M. Sarlotte. High Data Rate Fully Flexible SDR Modem. In *IEEE International Conference on Design Automation and Test in Europe (DATE)*, pages 1040–1044. IEEE, 2009.

[61] Paul Kaufmann and Marco Platzner. Toward Self-adaptive Embedded Systems: Multi-objective Hardware Evolution. In *20th International Conference on Architecture of Computing Systems (ARCS)*, volume 4415 of *LNCS*, pages 199–208. Springer, Mar 2007.

[62] Ariane Keller, Theus Hossmann, Martin May, Ghazi Bouabene, Christophe Jelger, and Christian F. Tschudin. A System Architecture for Evolving Protocol Stacks. In *International Conference on Computer Communications and Networks (ICCCN)*, pages 144–150. IEEE, 2008. Invited Paper.

[63] Angelos D. Keromytis, Jason L. Wright, Theo De Raadt, and Matthew Burnside. Cryptography as an Operating System Service: A Case Study. *ACM Transactions on Computer Systems*, 24(1):1–38, 2006.

[64] Paul Kohout, Brinda Ganesh, and Bruce Jacob. Hardware Support for Real-Time Operating Systems. In *1st IEEE/ACM/IFIP International Conference on Hardware/Software Codesign and System Synthesis (CODES+ISSS)*, pages 45–51, New York, NY, USA, 2003. ACM.

[65] Krzysztof Kosciuszkiewicz, Fearghal Morgan, and Krzysztof Kepa. Run-Time Management of Reconfigurable Hardware Tasks Using Embedded Linux. In *IEEE International Conference on Field-Programmable Technology (FPT)*, pages 209–215. IEEE, 2007.

[66] Chidamber Kulkarni, Gordon Brebner, and Graham Schelle. Mapping a Domain Specific Language to a Platform FPGA. In *Design Automation Conference*, volume 0, pages 924–927, Los Alamitos, CA, USA, 2004. IEEE.

[67] H. Lange and A. Koch. Low-Latency High-Bandwidth HW/SW Communication in a Virtual Memory Environment. In *IEEE International Conference on Field Programmable Logic and Applications (FPL)*, pages 281–286. IEEE, Aug 2008.

[68] ARM Limited. The AMBA 2.0 Specification. Website, 2010. `http://www.arm.com/products/solutions/AMBA_Spec.html`.

[69] R. Lipsett, E. Marschner, and M. Shahdad. VHDL – The Language. *IEEE Design & Test of Computers*, pages 28–41, Apr 1986.

[70] C. L. Liu and James W. Layland. Scheduling algorithms for multi-programming in a hard-real-time environment. *Journal of the ACM*, 20(1):46–61, 1973.

[71] P. Lysaght, B. Blodget, J. Mason, J. Young, and B. Bridgford. Invited Paper: Enhanced Architectures, Design Methodologies and CAD Tools for Dynamic Reconfiguration of Xilinx FPGAs. In *IEEE International Conference on Field Programmable Logic and Applications (FPL)*, pages 1–6. IEEE, Aug 2006.

[72] Patrick Lysaght and John Dunlop. Dynamic Reconfiguration of FPGAs. *More FPGAs*, 1993.

[73] Mateusz Majer, Jürgen Teich, Ali Ahmadinia, and Christophe Bobda. The Erlangen Slot Machine: A Dynamically Reconfigurable FPGA-based Computer. *The Journal of VLSI Signal Processing*, 47(1):15–31, Apr 2007.

[74] Robert Meiche. FPGA/CPU Multicore-Plattform für ReconOS/eCos. Diploma thesis, Universität Paderborn, 2009.

[75] M. Meissner, U. Kanus, G. Wetekam, J. Hirche, A. Ehlert, W. Strasser, M. Doggett, P. Forthmann, and R. Proksa. VIZARD II: A Reconfigurable Interactive Volume Rendering System. In *ACM SIGGRAPH/EUROGRAPHICS Conference on Graphics Hardware (HWWS)*, pages 137–146. Eurographics Association, 2002.

[76] Pedro Merino, Juan Carlos Lopez, and Margarida Jacome. A Hardware Operating System for Dynamic Reconfiguration of FPGAs. In *IEEE International Conference on Field Programmable Logic and Applications (FPL)*, pages 431–435. Springer-Verlag, 1998.

[77] Guerric Meurice de Dormale and Jean-Jacques Quisquater. High-Speed Hardware Implementations of Elliptic Curve Cryptography: a Survey. *Journal on Systems Architecture*, 53(2-3):72–84, 2007.

[78] J-Y. Mignolet, S. Vernalde, D. Verkest, and R. Lauwereins. Enabling Hardware-Software Multitasking on a Reconfigurable Computing Platform for Networked Portable Multimedia Appliances. In *2nd International Conference on Engineering of Reconfigurable Systems and Algorithms (ERSA)*, pages 116–122. CSREA Press, 2002.

[79] Mind NV. Release of the eCos Port to the Xilinx Virtex4 ML403 board. Website, 2008. http://www.mind.be/?page=ML403.

[80] Ana Lúcia De Moura and Roberto Ierusalimschy. Revisiting Coroutines. *ACM Transactions on Programming Languages and Systems (TOPLAS)*, 31(2):1–31, 2009.

[81] W.A. Najjar, W. Bohm, B.A. Draper, J. Hammes, R. Rinker, J.R. Beveridge, M. Chawathe, and C. Ross. High-Level Language Abstraction for Reconfigurable Computing. *IEEE Computer*, 36(8):63–69, Aug 2003.

[82] Jörg Niklas. Eine Monitoring- und Debugging-Infrastruktur für hybride HW/SW-Systeme. Student thesis, Universität Paderborn, 2008.

[83] V. Nollet, P. Coene, D. Verkest, S. Vernalde, and R. Lauwereins. Designing an Operating System for a Heterogeneous Reconfigurable SoC. In *International Parallel and Distributed Processing Symposium (IPDPS), Reconfigurable Architectures Workshop (RAW)*. IEEE, 2003.

[84] Open Verilog International (OVI). Verilog Hardware Description Language Reference Manual, Version 1.0, 1996.

[85] OpenCores. WISHBONE System-on-Chip (SoC) Interconnection Architecture for Portable IP Cores. Technical report, OpenCores Organization, 2002. http://opencores.org/downloads/wbspec_b3.pdf.

[86] Wesley Peck, Erik Anderson, Jason Agron, Jim Stevens, Fabrice Baijot, and David Andrews. hthreads: A Computational Model for Reconfigurable Devices. In *16th IEEE International Conference on Field Programmable Logic and Applications (FPL)*, volume 1, pages 885–888. IEEE, Aug 2006.

[87] Rodolfo Pellizzoni and Marco Caccamo. Real-Time Management of Hardware and Software Tasks for FPGA-Based Embedded Systems. *IEEE Transactions on Computers*, 56(12):1666–1678, Dec 2007.

[88] PetaLogix. Petalinux. Website, 2007. http://developer.petalogix.com/.

[89] Quadros Systems Inc. RTXC 3.2 real-time kernel. Website, 2007. `http://www.quadros.com/products/operating-systems/rtxc-32/`.

[90] Waldemar Reisch. Bildverarbeitungs-Architekturen und -Bibliotheken für das rekonfigurierbare Betriebssystem ReconOS. Diploma thesis, Universität Paderborn, 2007.

[91] L. M. Reyneri, F. Cucinotta, A. Serra, and L. Lavagno. A Hardware/Software Co-Design Flow and Ip Library Based on Simulink. In *38th annual Design Automation Conference (DAC)*, pages 593–598, New York, NY, USA, 2001. ACM.

[92] Tavis Rudd. Cheetah - The Python-Powered Template Engine. Website, 2009. `http://www.cheetahtemplate.org/`.

[93] M. Rullmann and R. Merker. Synthesis of Efficiently Reconfigurable Datapaths for Reconfigurable Computing. In *IEEE International Conference on Field-Programmable Technology (FPT)*. IEEE, Jan 2008.

[94] M. Rullmann, S. Siegel, and R. Merker. Optimization of Reconfiguration Overhead by Algorithmic Transformations and Hardware Matching. In *19th IEEE International Parallel and Distributed Processing Symposium (IPDPS)*, pages 151–156. IEEE, 2005.

[95] Secret Lab Technologies Ltd. Linux on Xilinx Virtex. Website, 2008. `http://wiki.secretlab.ca/index.php/Linux_on_Xilinx_Virtex`.

[96] N. Shirazi, W. Luk, and P.Y.K. Cheung. Run-Time Management of Dynamically Reconfigurable Designs. In *IEEE International Conference on Field Programmable Logic and Applications (FPL)*, pages 59–68. Springer-Verlag, 1998.

[97] H. Simmler, L. Levinson, and R. Männer. Multitasking on FPGA Coprocessors. In *IEEE International Conference on Field Programmable Logic and Applications (FPL)*, pages 121–130. Springer-Verlag, 2000.

[98] Alexandre Skyrme, Noemi Rodriguez, and Roberto Ierusalimschy. Exploring Lua for Concurrent Programming. *Journal of Universal Computer Science*, 14(21), 2008.

[99] Hayden Kwok-Hay So and Robert W. Brodersen. Improving Usability of FPGA-based Reconfigurable Computers through Operating System Support. In *16th IEEE International Conference on Field Programmable Logic and Applications (FPL)*, pages 349–354. IEEE, 2006.

[100] Hayden Kwok-Hay So, Artem Tkachenko, and Robert Brodersen. A Unified Hardware/software Runtime Environment for FPGA-based Reconfigurable Computers using BORPH. In *4th International Conference on Hardware/Software Codesign and System Synthesis (CODES+ISSS)*, pages 259–264. ACM Press, 2006.

[101] William Stallings. *Operating Systems: Internals and Design Principles, Sixth Edition*, chapter 2.2, pages 55–64. Prentice Hall, 2009.

[102] Christoph Steiger, Herbert Walder, and Marco Platzner. Operating Systems for Reconfigurable Embedded Platforms: Online Scheduling of Real-time Tasks. *IEEE Transactions on Computers*, 53(11):1392–1407, Nov 2004.

[103] Andrew S. Tanenbaum. *Structured Computer Organization, Fifth Edition*, chapter 8.1.2, pages 556–562. Prentice Hall, 2006.

[104] J. Teich, S. Fekete, and J. Schepers. Optimization of Dynamic Hardware Reconfigurations. *The Journal of Supercomputing*, 19(1):57–75, May 2000.

[105] The MathWorks, Inc. Simulink HDL Coder. Website, 2009. `http://www.mathworks.de/products/slhdlcoder/`.

[106] James E. Thornton. Considerations in Computer Design – Leading up to the Control Data 6600. Technical report, Control Data Chippewa Laboratory, 1963.

[107] M. Vuletić, L. Pozzi, and P. Ienne. Seamless Hardware-software Integration in Reconfigurable Computing Systems. *IEEE Design and Test of Computers*, 22(2):102–113, Mar 2005.

[108] Herbert Walder, Samuel Nobs, and Marco Platzner. XF-BOARD: A Prototyping Platform for Reconfigurable Hardware Operating Systems. In *4th International Conference on Engineering of Reconfigurable Systems and Algorithms (ERSA)*. CSREA Press, 2004.

[109] Herbert Walder and Marco Platzner. Reconfigurable Hardware Operating Systems: From Design Concepts to Realizations. In *3rd International Conference on Engineering of Reconfigurable Systems and Algorithms (ERSA)*, pages 248–287. CSREA Press, Jun 2003.

[110] G. Wigley and D. Kearney. The Development of an Operating System for Reconfigurable Computing. In *IEEE Symposium on FPGAs for Custom Computing Machines (FCCM)*. IEEE, 2001.

[111] Benedikt Wildenhain. Implementierung von Kryptographie-Hardware-beschleunigern für das HW/SW-Betriebssystem ReconOS. Bachelor's thesis, Universität Paderborn, 2008.

[112] J. A. Williams, N. W. Bergmann, and X. Xie. FIFO Communication Models in Operating Systems for Reconfigurable Computing. In *13th IEEE Symposium on Field-Programmable Custom Computing Machines (FCCM)*, pages 277–278. IEEE, 2005.

[113] Wind River. VxWorks 6.x. Website, 2007. http://www.windriver.com/products/run-time_technologies/Real-Time_Operating_Systems/VxWorks_6x/.

[114] Xin Xie, John Williams, and Neil Bergmann. Asymmetric Multi-Processor Architecture for Reconfigurable System-on-Chip and Operating System Abstractions. In *IEEE International Conference on Field-Programmable Technology, (FPT)*, pages 41–48. IEEE, 2007.

[115] Xilinx Inc. Bus Functional Model (BFM) Simulation of Processor Intellectual Property. Application Note, May 2006. XAPP516.

[116] Xilinx Inc. CoolRunner-II CPLD Family Data Sheet. Data Sheet, Sep 2008. DS090.

[117] Xilinx Inc. Early Access Partial Reconfiguration User Guide. User Guide, Sep 2008. UG208.

[118] Xilinx Inc. Virtex-4 FPGA User Guide. User Guide, Dec 2008. UG070.

[119] Xilinx, Inc. System Generator for DSP. Website, 2009. http://www.xilinx.com/tools/sysgen.htm.

[120] X. Zhang and K. Ng. A Review of High-Level Synthesis for Dynamically Reconfigurable FPGAs. *Microprocessors and Microsystems*, Jan 2000.

[121] Bin Zhou, Yingning Peng, and David Hwang. Pipeline FFT Architectures Optimized for FPGAs. *International Journal of Reconfigurable Computing*, 2009, 2009.

[122] L. Zhuo and V. Prasanna. High-Performance Designs for Linear Algebra Operations on Reconfigurable Hardware. *IEEE Transactions on Computers*, Jan 2008.